Retirement Sparks Redux

Looking Back and
Moving Forward

Other published work from Elaine M. Decker

70 Things To Do When You Turn 70 October 2013
Contributing author
ISBN-13: 978-1416209157

Retirement Sparks Again December 2012
More Humorous Reflections on Retirement
Paperback
ISBN-13: 978-1481192361

CANCER: A Coping Guide September 2012
For Those with the Big C
and Those Who Love Them
Paperback
ISBN-13: 978-1479226511

Retirement Sparks December 2011
Reigniting the Passion for Life—
Irreverent Observations on Retirement
Paperback
ISBN-13: 978-1468095708

New York Times

New Jersey Opinion: Sep 18, 1988
"Please Send One Bag of Garbage"
http://www.nytimes.com/1988/09/18/nyregion/new-jersey-opinion-
please-send-one-bag-of-garbage.html

New Jersey Opinion: July 17, 1988
"Commuter Calls It Quits"
http://www.nytimes.com/1988/07/17/nyregion/new-jersey-opinion-
commuter-calls-it-quits.html

And Other Articles in The Privacy Journal and Marketing News

Retirement Sparks Redux

Looking Back and
Moving Forward

Elaine M. Decker

by Elaine M. Decker

Published by Business Theatre Unlimited

ISBN-13: 978-1505428933   ISBN-10: 1505428939

*To those who have
expressed their enjoyment
in reading Retirement Sparks books,
my column in
Rhode Island's Prime Time
and my blog
retirementsparks.blogspot.com…*

*You've provided the fuel
for my decision
to use my retirement as a gateway
to becoming a serious writer.*

Contents

Contents (cont.)

Contents (cont.)

Page

Contents (cont.)

Page

Introduction

As I gathered material for this, the third book in my *Retirement Sparks* series, my husband and I were finally settling into a somewhat downsized condo. We were a long time getting here. Let me tell you why.

Retirement is a process, and a complicated one at that. I officially retired in April 2011. By that, I mean I stopped going to an office every day (and stopped receiving a regular paycheck). I immediately dove into what turned out to be an almost full-time job preparing our Victorian house for sale.

Retirement was supposed to enable me to follow my dream of becoming a serious writer. That presumed I'd have considerable free time and a level of financial stability to not need a "real" job. Here's what I've learned looking back on my first three years of retirement.

Until Fall 2014, there was no free time, and financial stability was elusive. Or at least predictability was. As Gilda Radner would say, "it's always something" to be fixed. And that's not just in a 100-plus year-old house you're selling. The condo we've been in for three months is also prone to things that go bump in the night. And I don't mean my husband as he gropes his way to our still-unfamiliar bathroom in the dark.

Getting back to the sale of our Victorian. The staging process took months. (It turns out staging is a euphemism for ruthless decluttering.) This can be challenging at best. For someone who has spent her life collecting things "just in case" they might come in handy, it's traumatic. Deciding which of two items to keep and which to part with made me feel like I had wandered into a Sophie's Choice world. (See my June 22 and October 19, 2013 posts on these topics in the Retirement Lifestyles section.)

I said goodbye to furniture that had served me faithfully for decades. I bungled my way through my first yard sale, leaving me with carloads of leftover goods to donate. When the house didn't sell, I replaced the old oil furnace with a new gas one and settled in for another "wicked" Rhode Island winter. And somehow I published my first book, *Retirement Sparks*.

Over the next two years, I had more wallpaper removed and walls re-plastered and painted. I managed to find time to continue blogging, to write a monthly column in a Rhode Island newspaper, and to publish two more books— *Retirement Sparks Again* and *Cancer: A Coping Guide*. I also wrote and collected enough material for my fourth book, *Retirement Sparks Redux*, which you are reading now.

We sold the house in June 2014 and moved temporarily to a sublet in a third floor walk-up with no AC. Also no land line and no Internet access. That interim move meant a two-pronged process: deciding what could go into storage for a few months and what we'd need for the summer. Like eight box fans. July 2014 was so hot in Providence that Luke, our elderly cat, spent most of the month on the bottom of the bathtub. There were many days that I was tempted to join him there.

Instead, I did a lot of reading, especially books on the writing process. On that subject, I highly recommend Dani Shapiro's book: *Still Writing*. My April 12, 2014 post, "Are You Still (Fill in the Blank)" in the Retirement Lifestyles section, was inspired by the book (and someone's comment to me in the local market).

We moved into our blissfully quiet Connecticut condo over Labor Day weekend. I've spent several months sorting through the packing boxes from storage and the sublet. Remembering which items were packed where has been daunting. Some items still elude me.

I've turned my attention to writing and to finally publishing *Retirement Sparks Redux*. I'm exploring styles that are different from my usual social satire—styles that are more personal but less humorous. You'll find these posts in the last section of this book: Wistful Reflections. As the final entry indicates, in *Retirement Sparks Redux*, I'm continuing to write what I know. I'm just not telling all. Yet.

Retirement Sparks Redux

Section I

Retirement Lifestyles

Signs You Need A Retirement Hobby

Original Post Date May 3, 2013

Two years into my retirement it hit me: I really need to find a new hobby. There are a number of signs you should recognize if you've also reached that point.

The sign that really brought this home to me had to do with watching TV, and not just any TV.

√ You watch so much Retro TV in the afternoon that *Gunsmoke*, *Bonanza* and *The Big Valley* are now in reruns.

Reruns of reruns. Really? How pathetic is that? And if that's not bad enough:

√ You know exactly how the rabbit ears need to be positioned for each of the 12 channels your TV can receive so you get the best reception for each one.

Then there are the telltale signs that have to do with making things into projects.

√ You've written down the steps you go through when you put on your walking shoes. "Get shoes. Loosen laces. Pull out tongue. Get yard-long shoehorn. Insert shoehorn. Insert foot. Straighten tongue. Tighten laces. Tie laces: *right-over-left, left-over-right, makes a square knot, good and tight.*" Repeat.

√ You've darned three dozen socks in the past two months. Some of your darning has been re-darned.

√ You check the bottom of your husband's clothes closet, hoping to find some laundry that needs to be done.

Even those who are avid readers and consider having more time to read during retirement to be a hobby might need to find a new one. Recognize any of these?

√ When you sit down to read a book, you fall asleep in ten minutes.

√ You check your email every half hour.

√ You wait at the front door for the mailman and hope he has several text-dense catalogues you can read— page by page.

√ You memorized the second edition of *Excel for Dummies*, even though it's 17 years out of date.

Some other signs reflect a lack of focus. Or compulsive behavior. Or both.

√ You stare at the 7-day vitamin container each morning, trying to remember what day it is. (And your spouse is no help at all.)

√ You feed your cat four times a day. Lately he's been hiding under the bed when he hears you coming up the stairs in the middle of the afternoon.

√ You prepare a detailed shopping list at least twice a week, even though you go for groceries only once. You count the number of eggs in the carton three times before you remember to write down whether you need to buy them or not. Then you leave the list on the kitchen table when you finally go shopping. So you buy more eggs, just in case. You now have four cartons in the fridge. Two of them are partially used.

Oh, yes. Most of us can't wait to be retired. All that extra time on our hands! But be careful what you wish for. Or else get some great recipes for egg salad. And adopt a few more cats.

Peripatetic Retirees
Original Post Date May 25, 2013

Ever the optimist, I'm looking ahead to how my husband and I will spend our time together once we're truly retired. This presumes that I'm eventually successful in dragging him away from his store. Since we're looking to downsize outside of Rhode Island, I've pretty much got that problem covered. In theory, we'll have side-by-side office space where he'll work on the web version of his store and I'll continue to write and to develop some web properties that have been percolating for years.

If you've been following my blog, you know that the prospect of a life of nothing but writing and web activity is already beginning to lose its luster for me. Those who know Jagdish keep asking how he'll survive without his stool and his "ashram." I think I've found the perfect solution to both these issues.

We're going to take our act—or more correctly acts—on the road. We'll get an Airstream or Winnebago RV (or whatever the generic is) and travel across the country. This will enable us to see states where we've never been, or only breezed through on business. We'll spend time in the interesting cities that folks have been recommending to us. And we'll sniff out places where we can hawk our wares and ply our trade.

The first step will be to buy a used RV. The ones in Texas, Arkansas and Missouri seem to be more affordable, but we'd have to travel to get them; catch 22. I figure we'll need to spend around $50,000 if we want to buy it here on the East Coast. This means that the home we downsize to needs to be at least $50,000 less expensive than what is currently in our budget. It also must be somewhere that will allow us to park the RV in the driveway. (Can you say: *"You might be a redneck if..."*?)

We'll need a portable peddler's cart—the kind you see at craft fairs or on sidewalks in the summer in tourist areas. Most of it will be filled with products from SPECTRUM-India, Jagdish's retail store. He'll have incense, essential oils, wind chimes, singing bowls and more. A portion of the cart will feature my books. I'll do readings every hour, hoping to lure folks into buying the book after they hear how witty and funny I am. Jagdish will do handwriting analysis, palm readings and henna tattoos.

We'll spend a week or two in each location, working our way from East to West and back again, following the change of seasons, as appropriate. This way, Jagdish can "set up shop" in all the places that visitors to SPECTRUM-India have been promoting to him over the years, without having to commit to a long-term lease. He'll be able to take his stool with him, but he won't be able to sit there until midnight or later. I'll get to talk to him all day, and even eat meals with him. What a concept!

We'll become peripatetic retirees, wandering the country like eccentric vagabonds. Jagdish will be able to hold court with different people every week. His friends back in Rhode Island won't have to worry about him having store withdrawal. He'll be like a turtle, carrying his store on his back, in a manner of speaking. I'll continue to gather pop culture to write about, but with an even broader geographic perspective.

Our list of destinations will be chock full of university towns and artists' communities. Our peddler's cart will have stickers from Burlington, Amherst, Charlottesville, Chapel Hill, and Austin. We'll spend time in Camden, Asheville, St. Augustine, Taos, Santa Fe and Albuquerque. We'll camp out in Savannah, New Orleans, and Mill Valley. If we hit the weather right, we'll stop in Madison, Boulder, and Portland, OR.

Our peddler's cart will have so many miles on it, we'll have to buy new tires every few months. (Note to self: add tire expense to budget.) At the end of each year, we'll evaluate the places we've been. We'll return to the "keepers" the next year and explore new locales to replace the slots vacated by the losers. We'll take suggestions of cities to add from any and all sources. We'll shamelessly mooch meals from people we know in an area and folks we meet along the way.

After a few years, we might even decide to relocate to one of the perpetual winners, especially if it's more affordable than where we've initially downsized. Oh, yes! This is a plan devised at the peak of my creative genius, and without the lubricant of even one glass of wine. Imagine what I might come up with after a glass or two! Or perhaps don't.

Just-In-Case Lifestyle

Original Post Date Jun. 22, 2013

You may have heard of the Just-In-Time inventory concept popularized several decades back. To reduce costs, manufacturers kept the absolute minimum inventory on hand. They implemented computer systems to help predict orders and locate production facilities to optimize their ability to deliver goods "just in time."

Today, thanks to digital printing, that concept has found its way into publishing as "Print On Demand." That's how I published my four books, through Amazon's Create Space arm. My books get printed only when someone orders one of them on Amazon.com. Don't worry. This essay is not about selling my books. It's about the contrarian inventory concept of "Just In Case," which means it's about how I came to have such an array of belongings.

"Just In Case" is a mantra that I've lived by most of my life. It explains half the clothes that are in my closet, tags still attached. Also a cabinet full of cake pans, just in case I decide to take up baking. And shelves of *How To…* books and file drawers of reference materials on arcane topics. In preparation for downsizing our house, I've been weeding out things I acquired "just in case." Not an easy task when you've spent your life accumulating stuff.

I blame my mother for this. She had a full-size standing freezer in our kitchen that was always chock full of meals she'd prepared, ready to be defrosted at a moment's notice. She did this—you guessed it—just in case a platoon of friends or relatives dropped in unannounced and needed to be fed. Or more accurately, just in case they dropped in unannounced, period. It was her assumption that people always needed to be fed. (Did I mention my mother was Italian?)

My brother turned this into a standing joke with her. As my mother aged into her eighties, she'd engage us in conversations about who should take what from the house after she was "gone." When my brother was visiting from California and she started on this, he would ask her teasingly: *"Where're you going, Mom?"* And she'd shoot back: *"Well, I won't be around forever, you know."*

This prompted him to reply: *"You're not going to leave us anytime soon. You wouldn't do that to us."* She'd ask what made him so sure, and he'd point out that the freezer was not completely filled to the brim. *"You wouldn't leave us with the freezer partly empty. How would we feed all the people who'd be coming back to the house after your funeral?"* Then we'd all laugh, and my mother would get up and start cooking.

It wasn't only with food that she believed in being prepared. She kept brand new pajamas and a robe in her dresser, just in case she had to go to the hospital unexpectedly. So you see, it's mostly my mother's fault that I've been saddled with this "just in case" mentality.

To be fair, I suppose my father is also partly to blame. He amassed a garage full of tools, just in case. We lived in one of the snowiest parts of New Jersey, but our car spent the winters in our driveway. There was no room for it in the garage. In his defense, my father used most of his tools and equipment. Or again, more accurately, he used them or he loaned them out to neighbors.

He had a table saw and a band saw and a wall full of those plastic organizers with pull-out drawers. He had drivers for every type of screw ever made and wrenches that looked like pieces of bent metal. Back in the fifties I was probably the only teenage girl who knew what an Allen wrench was. I was also the only freshman in my college dorm who arrived with her own toolbox. I became popular quite quickly. (Thank you, Dad.)

Between them, my parents were prepared for every eventuality that could have befallen our household. I was doomed from the get go. Even now, I stock up on extra candles, batteries and bottled water, in case the power goes out for a few days. That was a common occurrence where I grew up, but it hasn't happened once in my twenty years in Providence. Not even the year when Connecticut was a disaster.

No, a Shaker lifestyle was never in my cards. Speaking of cards, I have two decks (unused) especially for playing Briscola. You never know when you're going to run into some Italians who might want to play that card game, so I bought the decks when I was in Piemonte. Just in case.

Briscola cards from Trieste and Naples

Liar, Liar, Pants on Fire

Original Post Date Jul. 6, 2013

I recently read Ellen Degeneres' book *Seriously... I'm Kidding.* In one chapter, she wrote about the lies we all tell. An example she used: you're on your way out the door to work when you notice a stain on your shirt. You're too lazy to change, so you tell everyone it happened on the way to the office.

While we all tell white lies, retirees tell more of them. Our lives are a petri dish of fibs. We also lie for different reasons than when we were younger. Young people are prone to one type of lie: the *Get Out of Trouble* one. It begins with "the dog ate my homework" and progresses to "we ran out of gas." (Remember what you were doing when you told that one?)

I've identified six types of lies that older folks tell. These do not include *Get Out of Trouble*, though at least one senior lie resembles that youthful one.

The first senior lie is the *Embarrassment/Matter of Pride* lie. Your daughter phones to check if you took your medicine that morning. "Of course I did," you reply, indignantly, on your way to fetch the day-of-week dosage container that has not yet been opened today. Although this resembles the youthful *Get Out of Trouble*, fear of getting into trouble isn't behind it. It's the embarrassment of admitting you once again forgot.

The second type is the *Ignorance/Forgetfulness* lie. The shuttle bus can take you to the local market every Tuesday at 10 am. Your neighbor asks why she didn't see you on it last week. "I didn't need to go to the market. I have everything I need," say you-of-the-empty-cupboard.

This is not the same as simply lying about something you forgot. With the medication example, you lied knowingly when confronted. The second type is done in complete innocence. You didn't know about the shuttle, or you forgot you ever knew. Rather than admit that, you fabricate a lie to divert the conversation elsewhere.

Type three becomes increasingly common as we age: the *Convenience* lie. Normally, I don't park in restricted areas, but lately I find it harder to resist convenience. The other day, I pulled into a "No Standing" zone in front of the bank so my husband could use the ATM. His knees are creaky and he uses a cane if he's going a considerable distance, but he's fine for shorter walks.

As he was leaving the car without his cane, I asked him to take it with him. "That way, if anyone says something to me about parking here, I'll tell them it's because my husband is an invalid." I could hear Ellen Degeneres chastising me: "Liar, Liar, pants on fire!" I guess my husband couldn't hear her, because he dutifully took his cane and pretended to hobble up the steps to the bank.

The fourth variation is *Delaying Tactics*. This buys time while you try to figure out (or remember) what's being asked of you. Women commonly use this by rooting through their purses, mumbling, "Hang on. It's in here somewhere." We're actually buying time while we try to remember where we put whatever is supposedly in our purse.

Type five is *Deflected Blame*, which is sometimes a companion to *Get Out of Trouble* or *Embarrassment*. I've blamed my cats for "scratches" and "claw marks" on my limbs and torso when my GP asked how I got them. I might have stabbed myself with a knife or scissors, but blaming the felines keeps him from lecturing me about my carelessness. Besides, it could have been the cats. Who knows?

This reminds me of one of my favorite movie scenes. It's from "*10*," where Dudley Moore is visiting the pastor to get information on the Bo Derek character. The housekeeper noisily passes gas as she bends over to set the serving tray on the coffee table and the dog races out of the room. The pastor explains: *"Whenever Mrs. Kissel breaks wind, we beat the dog."*

The sixth and final senior lie is *Keep In Practice*, which is just what it sounds like. Even with plenty of occasions to employ the other five types, it's a good idea to have a few of this last one in your hip pocket, just in case. "My doctor said that's not a good idea." (Be careful to never specify which doctor.) "I'm trying to de-clutter, so I packed it away in the attic (or donated it to Good Will.)" "Yes, I know you told me that, but I didn't realize you were serious."

If you think you're immune from telling any of these senior lies, feel free to proclaim your innocence. Chances are, no one will believe you anyway.

Sophie's Choice Decluttering

Original Post Date Oct. 19, 2013

One of my earliest posts dealt with the process of downsizing, especially figuring out what to keep and what to jettison. I confessed my weakness of anthropomorphizing objects, which made the process even more difficult. I imagined the floor lamp selected to be discarded saying: "Why me? Why not him? Why am I not as lovable? Look how interesting MY shade is! Just put a stronger bulb in me, for heaven's sake!"

As we get closer to moving to smaller living quarters (please, Lord), I'm once again rummaging through my closets to see what should stay and what should go. As I handle each item, I've found myself wandering down memory lane into a Sophie's Choice of decluttering.

It started with my bathrobes, something I seldom wear, but feel I should have, just in case. (There's that "just in case" again.) I found four of them. One is royal blue silk, kimono style, with a huge embroidered eagle on the back. It's the only knee length one; it's good for most travel needs; and it makes me feel exotic, so it's a keeper.

The next one is also kimono style. It's long and red (my favorite color) and it has embroidered scenes on the back and front. I bought it on a trip to San Francisco—part business, part pleasure. I coordinated the timing with my parents' visit to my brother. The robe came from Chinatown and it reminds me of the fun we had wandering the shops together.

My mother liked San Francisco, but not the morning fog, which she said left a funny smell that hung in the air over people's homes. By people, she meant my brother's pothead friends, in whose house we stayed. I can still hear my father telling them to put a saucer under the tomato plant on the end table, or else it would leave a ring. That reminded me of my brother's friend back in New Jersey, whose wife wondered why the "tomato plants" outside their garden apartment never bore any fruit.

I have another long, kimono style robe. It's also red, but it's polished cotton with printed flowers, and it washes beautifully. My brother-in-law gave it to me when I had my cancer surgery in Vermont. I'd been misdiagnosed for months in New Jersey, where I lived. My brother-in-law (a physician) networked me into an appointment with the best breast surgeon in Burlington for a second opinion. I eventually entered a National Institutes of Health study and had my initial treatment up there.

The fourth robe was a get-well gift from some close friends from my days at Colgate Palmolive. I remember wearing it in the hospital after my surgery. It's long and heavier—a rich cranberry jacquard, lined with turquoise terrycloth, which absorbs water nicely. It's perfect for cold weather mornings. It was also great to put on while I was doubled over from my surgery and unable to dry off thoroughly after my shower.

You might wonder why I'd want to keep things associated with serious health problems. Those last two robes remind me that I got through such a difficult time because of the love and support of family and friends. Parting with any of my robes, no matter how seldom I wear them, would be a Sophie's Choice dilemma—like deciding which of my children to give up.

After my bathrobe foray, I decided that clothes closets were not the best place to start this phase of decluttering. I moved downstairs to tackle some kitchen cabinets. Surely somewhere among the dozen or so flower vases were a few that could be parted with.

Well, not the Baccarat. That's the one my sister and her husband gave us for our wedding. It's a classic shape that works with both modern and traditional décor. Plus, it curves like waves, and I've put blue silk flowers in it to create positive "water" *feng shui* in our entry hall. And not the vase that Vivek and Anu gave us. That's the only one tall enough and heavy enough to corral a dozen roses. It's held many anniversary bouquets from my husband over the years.

You can guess where this is headed. No matter how long it takes to sell our house, I'm doomed to pack up and move with us cartons full of "children" I can't part with. Don't worry about where I'll put all of it. Basement storage is one of our down-sized condo must-haves. A wine cellar would be nice, too.

Yoga for Seniors

Original Post Date Nov. 30, 2013

Are you interested in lowering your BMI (Body Mass Index)? If your lingerie budget is as skimpy as mine post-retirement, before you spring for the caffeine panties I wrote about (see Section IV), you might want to look into yoga exercises. They not only relax you and tone your body, they're purported to help keep your weight under control.

There are quite a few exercises that shouldn't be too challenging for seniors, but would still provide benefits. Several of them can be done using chairs and walls, and therefore don't require us to get down on a mat. Or more importantly, to get up from one when we're done. However, most of the ones I'm sharing today have you at least partly on the floor. You can thank me later.

Yoga helps stretch our muscles, ligaments and tendons. It also improves our flexibility and increases our range of motion, all admirable objectives. According to *health.howstuffworks.com*, "you don't need to be able to tie yourself in knots to become more flexible." That's a relief. I always thought that true yogis needed the ability to turn themselves into pretzels. On that note, let's try some poses.

We're starting with the *One-legged Breaking Wind Pose* to help get rid of excess stomach gas. Lie on your back with arms and legs extended. Exhale, draw your knees to your chest and clasp your hands around them until you break wind. Straighten just your left leg, extending it along the floor. Then bring your left knee back to your chest and hold until you fart again. Release and extend your right leg. Bring your right knee back to your chest and exhale for one final wind breaker. I hope you feel better now.

Legs in Parentheses improves flexibility and has been adapted especially for seniors. Sit on the floor and spread your legs apart as much as you comfortably can. If you're able to straighten them quite widely, by all means, go for the traditional *Legs in V*. But feel free to bend your knees slightly into parentheses. Lean forward and feel your leg muscles stretching as you count to ten. Lean back. Repeat.

The *Shiva Shiver* is an obscure yoga pose that helps you lose weight. Supposedly, if you shiver for one hour, you burn 400 calories. Stand in front of your freezer in your underwear. Open the door and put your head inside. Within a few minutes, you should start to shiver. Stay like this for 15 minutes and you'll burn 100 calories. Hint: empty the freezer out first, in case you fall in, and set a timer to revive you when you're done. The Shiva Shiver gives new meaning to the phrase "freezer burn."

Quarter Spinal Twist is great for seniors with osteoporosis; it lengthens and strengthens your spine. So put on some Chubby Checker and let's do *The Twist*. Sit with the bottoms of your feet under your butt. Then place your left foot flat on the floor outside your right knee. If you can't reach the floor with your foot flat, touch with just your toe. Twist to the left a quarter turn until your foot comes off the floor, or until your muffin top pinches. Switch feet and legs and twist again.

One of my favorite positions is *Downward Facing Cat.* It helps us strengthen our abdominal and back muscles, improving our balance. Get down on all fours, like a cat. If you're not sure how this looks, go to your local animal shelter and adopt a cat. Bring it home and watch it for a few hours. Then stretch like your feline friend, rounding your spine, with your head down. *DoingA360.com/Basic-Yoga-Poses* says: "As you reverse this... the head comes up and the belly droops." Boy, have I got this position covered!

The unfortunately-named *Corpse* pose helps you relax at the end of your yoga session. I didn't need a website to tell me that. I doze off almost every time I do the *Corpse.* I just never had a name for it. *Climbing the Wall* is a variation for seniors. Lie on your back on the floor with legs straight up against a wall, arms slightly out from your sides. Then wiggle around. It's a good way to scratch your back when it's driving you crazy. It's also the end of our session.

Master these six yoga poses and you'll be well on your way to senior Nirvana, with lower blood pressure, better balance and improved flexibility. Some of you will also have a lower BMI and a new cat to keep you warm. I'm here to serve.

Bow Tie Renaissance

Original Post Date Feb. 8, 2014

A news feature that caught my attention reported on a surge in bow tie sales. They interviewed two young men who had purchased Beau Ties Limited of Vermont in late 2012 from an elderly gent who was retiring. He had wanted to sell his 'baby' to people who would nourish it as carefully as he had and keep the ties American-sourced and handmade. Based on the feature, he succeeded.

The sampling of silk prints I saw was mouthwatering and prompted me to do some research. I found a variety of bow-tie styles and ways to wear them. Since older gentlemen gravitate to the bow, I've put together a handy style reference guide. I won't be covering bow ties interpreted in wood or feathers. Likewise not hokey ones with blinking lights. And certainly not ones tied onto parts of the anatomy other than men's necks. (Sorry, ladies.)

When we hear "bow tie, " most of us picture **The Professor.** It's tied neatly, but it's often worn crooked, and with a tweed jacket. For reference, check out Harrison Ford in the earlier scenes in the first *Indiana Jones*, or David McCallum in the hit TV show *NCIS*.

We may also imagine **The Preppy Old-Boy** style, with its angled repp stripe a la Brooks Brothers. These come straight or with rakishly pointed ends.

The **Neck Pincher** is a poorly-worn variation of The Professor. Its most famous wearer is Paul Rubens, aka Pee Wee Herman. The pinching has nothing to do with the

thickness of the wearer's neck and it differs from the **Wattle Anchor** (see below). The Pincher is simply a bow tie worn too tightly or a tie that is far too small in proportion to the wearer's physique and appears to be pinching him.

Some interesting bow tie shapes are **The Butterfly**, **The Fan** and **The Poufy Gift Bow**. Note the features that differentiate them.

The **Butterfly** is a full style, usually with two soft bumps on each outer edge.

The **Fan** is often confused with The Butterfly, but The Fan has sharp folds and doesn't dip in the center of the outer edges.

The Poufy Gift Bow has three soft bumps, one of which may be almost imperceptible.

The Accordion is sometimes mistaken for The Fan, but it's a flatter style, with straighter edges. Sometimes The Accordion is actually flat but achieves the folded look through a printed pattern.

The **Wattle Anchor** is worn by men whose necks have given up trying to look good in any type of tie. When gentlemen reach this point, they often start wearing a bow tie at the base of their wattle, in hopes of directing attention away from the droop. Their shirt neck does not gap (yet). For reference, we have the midlife Winston Churchill (who always had a wattle), an ignominious to-be-nameless former president of Brown University, and Harrison Ford as Branch Rickey in the movie *42*.

Do not confuse The Wattle Anchor with **The Old Geezer**, our final style. Again, these are similar ties, but The Old Geezer is worn by men who have decided to give their wattle some breathing room. There is never a pinch of the neck with this later style, and not much of an attempt to hide the wattle. The tie is more of a celebration of it. Churchill in his later years converted to Old Geezers from his earlier

Wattle Anchors. The same tie can be used as a Wattle Anchor or as an Old Geezer, depending on how it's worn.

You may notice that I haven't mentioned clip-on ties. They're as bad as clip-on suspenders. If you don't feel qualified to tie a bow, have it tied by your haberdasher. Then have it converted to a strap that hooks at the back of your neck. It will be easy to put on and will look almost as good as the real thing.

But let's face it. There's no substitute for learning to properly tie a bow tie. It's like learning to pour a proper cup of tea or the perfect head on a draft beer. Or in my mind, pairing the right wine with dinner. On that note…

Perks of Retirement

Original Post Date Mar. 8, 2014

A post on a friend's Facebook page got me thinking about the perks of retirement. The friend isn't retired; she's still required to get out of bed every weekday to go to an office somewhere. That's part of what motivated her comment on this recent frigid morning. "I wished I could crawl back in bed, pull the covers over my head and hibernate until it's over."

My immediate reaction was: "Hibernation! What a great idea! Now that I'm retired, I could actually do that all winter if I really wanted to." It's not likely I'll choose to hibernate, but the option is there for me. At the very least, I can do that pull-the-covers-over-my-head thing. If I put out enough dry food and several bowls of fresh water for my cat, Luke, I could burrow like that for days. If it's really cold, I could probably get Luke to cuddle under there with me awhile. Double perk.

We're ready to list our house for sale (again). My real estate agent plans to stop by today to drop off some paperwork. Since I'm on the computer in my basement office, it will take me a few minutes to get upstairs to answer the door. I told her to call me when she's in front of the house so I can meet her at her car. (She's recovering from some surgery.) This put another perk of retirement into my head.

When I'm not expecting anyone, I don't have to answer the door if I'm busy or too lazy to go upstairs. Or downstairs. Or get up from the kitchen table. If it turns out it was someone I know—a friend or a neighbor, say—I can always tell her we must have been out of town. Retirees go out of town at the drop of a hat. Are relatives looking to visit for a few days and I don't want them around? I'll say we decided to head south to escape the snow. Or to see a city that's on our bucket list.

Retirees are expected to have a bucket list. One from which they're actively checking things off (before they check out). We don't have a bucket list, but this could be another perk of retirement. First, that we're entitled to lie about things, like being out of town and having lists of any kind. Second, that we can take the time to put together a bucket list. And then make and execute plans to tick things off. Or ignore it altogether. Whatever.

Some about-to-be-retirees look forward to having more time to cook. Perhaps to sign up for a couples' cooking class. Or take chefs' classes at *Le Cordon Bleu*. By the way, the website *Chefs.com* takes you to Le Cordon Bleu's *Bleu Ribbon Kitchen*. Not "Blue Ribbon." And not "*Bleu Ruban*." Aside from the inconsistency of languages used, isn't "*cordon*" just another French word for "ribbon"? It means "rope" or "cord," after all. So, Le Cordon Bleu *Bleu Ribbon Kitchen* is "the blue ribbon blue ribbon kitchen."

I find this annoying, but I digress. Getting back to perks. My retirement is a time to stock up the freezer with Kashi dinners and not feel guilty when I don't prepare proper meals three nights in a row. Or longer. Except for Luke's of course.

The more I think about them, the more I like these perks of retirement. Once we sell the house and downsize out of Rhode Island, the possibilities will increase. For one thing, I'll be able to get my husband away from his store. He still goes to work every morning and he's there about 90 hours a week. When that's in our rearview, we can enjoy the perks together. On frigid mornings, I might even get him to cuddle under the covers with Luke and me. There's one for my bucket list.

Are You Still
(Fill in the Blank)
Original Post Date April 12, 2014

I ran into an acquaintance (a fellow retiree) I hadn't seen in awhile and she asked me: *"Are you still writing?"* Looking back, I realize that I've finally "made it" as a writer when people ask if I'm still doing it. One of the books I asked Santa to bring me was *Still Writing*, by Dani Shapiro. I asked for several of them on the writing process, but I found *Still Writing* to be the most helpful.

Shapiro's title comes from the fact that folks tend not to take writing seriously as a career. They think of it as something one does in one's spare time, or that it's a sort of affliction. The question presumes there's a chance you might have gotten over it since the last time they saw you. Or given up, since you weren't likely to be good enough to get published. They don't understand that writers just have to write.

The more I thought about this, the more I realized that this is the situation for a lot of retirees, as well. People assume that something you take up in retirement automatically falls into the hobby category. It doesn't occur to them that it might be a second act for you. They'll ask you questions they would never pose to someone in his forties or fifties.

A college classmate in Canada took up clarinet late in life. In her retirement, she plays in several local bands. At our last reunion, she went home a day early so she could participate in the first concert of the spring series. She added tenor saxophone to her repertoire so she could join the jazz group. Her Facebook page is filled with posts about upcoming gigs and performances that were well received. Her music is more than simply a way to while away free time. It's life affirming for her.

Maybe you'll decide to study a foreign language. Do that when you're forty-something, and your friends won't consider saying: *"Are you still trying to learn Mandarin?"* But once you've become a senior citizen, they'll assume you'll dabble for a few lessons and move on to something less challenging. Just ignore them. Leave a few copies of the *Guangzhou Daily* on your cocktail table the next time they drop by for coffee. Then mention you're now also studying Cantonese.

Another of my college classmates is taking advantage of time freed up after she stopped working full time to become a Master Gardener. The qualification process is demanding and complex. She plans to volunteer as a guide and lecturer at the United States Botanic Garden once she has her credentials. That's not exactly piddling away her free time. So if you run into her, don't ask: *"Are you still working on identifying those weeds you're pulling out of your flower bed?"*

It's not unusual for a man to use his retirement to launch a woodworking business. Carpentry might have been a hobby when he was employed elsewhere. Now his workshop is not just his haven but also a source of discretionary income. And then some. *"Are you still making those rocking horses for your grandkids?"* Yup. For his grandkids, and those of dozens of other grandparents. You can put your name on the waiting list—for delivery next year. He's about to leave on a month-long trip to Bali.

Speaking of travel, another college friend and his wife have finally retired so they can start a tour business. They own a home in Southern France and they're specializing in tours of the Secret Provence. I can see a lot of tax advantages in this, since it's well beyond the hobby stage. What I can't see is someone asking them: *"Are you still doing that tour thingy?"*

Retired presidents almost always move on to another career. George H. W. Bush has become internationally recognized as a senior statesman. Bill Clinton is now thought of as a philanthropist instead of a philanderer. Bush the younger ("Dubya") recently had a showing of his paintings of famous people. He's taking art classes and seems serious about making this his post-presidential act. He also seems to have enough talent that I doubt anyone will dare ask him in five years: *"Are you still painting?"*

From now on, when I run into someone who says: *"Are you still writing?"* I plan to smile and answer yes. Then I'll add, ever so sweetly: *"Are you still reading?"* and hand them a business card with the URL for my blog and the titles of all the books I've published.

Retirement Sparks Redux

Section II

Retirement Stresses and
Pet Peeves

Retirement Plagues—
Sneezing Fits, Bug Bites and Bruises

Original Post Date May 11, 2013

Lately I'm prone to a rash of plagues, or a plague of rashes, or both. They've come upon me like carpenter ants on a vine-covered porch since I've been retired.

Every year around this time, I get little bug bites that itch like crazy. They start at my ankles and work their way up my body over a few weeks. Places on my lower back that are hard to reach are a favorite snacking area for these critters. Also the wing flaps of my upper arms. For immediate relief, I scrub my skin to within an inch of its life with the back brush in the shower.

I also treat with my father's go-to ointment—Boroleum. It's an analgesic with menthol and eucalyptol. It was developed for nasal use, but it's versatile. Remember the dad in *My Big Fat Greek Wedding* who used Windex on everything, including zits? Well, that's me with my Boroleum, thanks to my father. It's amazingly soothing, but only for awhile. No matter what I do, until the nibbling season is over, I'm doomed to a life of itch and scratch.

This is also the season for sneezing fits. Those with severe allergies are thinking: "Big whoop. The whole year is that season for me." I understand the need to sneeze when I'm exposed to pollen. But my office is in the basement. In a windowless area. The fits I get there at this time of year go on and on.

The first sneeze, I just ignore. The second sneeze gets me looking around for the tissue box, just in case. By the third sneeze, I'm trying to sniff the drips back up there. Sneeze four gets me pressing my knees together. Sneeze five has me blowing my nose (still pressing my knees together). And blowing. And blowing. By the time sneeze six comes around, and it usually does, I'm running up the stairs to the bathroom.

Maybe my office gets dustier in Spring. It doesn't seem that way to me. True, I drag the porch furniture out of the basement around the same time, and that stirs things up. But they're in a different room and they go out the bulkhead. Even Luke is sneezing more now, and he hasn't been o-u-t in weeks. Whatever the reason, sneeze fests are just another plague of the season for us.

My recent checkup with my GP reminded me of yet another side effect of an aging body: I bruise much more easily now. I guess my skin is thinner, so the blood vessels are closer to the surface. You know those little suction cup electrodes the tech sticks onto you when she does your annual EKG? Now they leave red marks. They usually disappear within a few hours, but it's a different story for the other bruises that I get without having a clue why.

The other day I found a small discoloration on my left forearm. I'm sure it started as a typical black and blue mark. By the time I noticed it, the color had already moved on to the green phase. Now it's that ugly yellow that signals the end of the cycle. I find bruises on my hips and thighs all the time, and I rarely can remember bumping into anything. Or more correctly, into anything in particular.

I bump into things all the time. My depth perception has always been lousy. Now that my eyesight is also less than stellar, unintentional contact with my surroundings happens several times a day, leaving me muttering: "Ouch! That's going to leave a mark." The more I walk around the house, the more bruises I get, and at least half of the ones I notice have origins unknown.

This provides a suitable excuse for just staying put in a chair with a good book. And a nice glass of wine. And no, it's not the wine that makes me clumsy, so you can wipe that smirk off your face. What's even better—by the second glass, I don't notice the bug bites anymore. Ah, Spring! When one's thoughts turn to restocking the "medicine cabinet" with Boroleum and tissues. And wine, of course.

Changing Tastes

Original Post Date Jun. 15, 2013

When I did our grocery shopping this week, the type of yoghurt we prefer was nowhere to be found in the local Stop & Shop, a major chain. I usually buy their store brand, but I'll pay extra for Stonyfield, if that's the only way I can get the variation we use. That is: regular yoghurt, nonfat, plain, in the large container.

There was exactly one regular S&S yoghurt in the large container, and it was nonfat vanilla. We don't like the vanilla. The Stonyfield section had several nonfat vanilla ones, and exactly one plain, but it was low fat. I snapped it up anyway, to avoid having to stop at another market. In case you're not a yoghurt eater, let me tell you why our variation is so hard to find these days. Everyone has hopped onto the Greek yoghurt bandwagon. It's thicker and creamier, but we prefer regular. My husband, Jagdish, won't touch the Greek.

This episode made me realize yet again that people's tastes change over time, and because of that, food and beverages that I've enjoyed for years are suddenly difficult, if not impossible to find. I'm sorry, but the older I get, the more I appreciate some stability in my life. I resent having to rejigger my eating habits to keep up with what's in vogue this month.

In rare instances, the world's tastes have caught up with my own. I was a tea drinker when tea wasn't cool. Now even Starbucks is pushing the teacart. This means I have more varieties from which to choose and every place I shop has a decent supply. Oh, yes, and there's usually one brand on sale somewhere. Sweet!

One beverage where tastes have changed notably over the years, including my own, is wine. I've always gone for drier wines, but I used to prefer white. (These days I prefer red.) I remember when Chablis was the wine of choice when you went out to dinner. Now I rarely see Chablis on a wine list, unless it's three pages long.

Likewise no longer easy to find is Verdicchio, which was one of my youthful preferences. I loved that citrusy zing and the interesting bottles, especially the cute fish-shaped one and the curvy number. Speaking of the curvy bottle (Fazi Battaglia), I also loved their radio commercials, the ones where diners struggled to pronounce the name. "Bring us some of that Fuzzy Baggies" is particularly memorable.

Mateus was another popular option in the early seventies, an affordable rosé that has pretty much disappeared (mercifully). Most folks pronounced it Mahtoose, but I always gave it three syllables, like Matthew in Portuguese— Mah-teh-oos. Apparently, the pronunciation, like the wine, targets a less-urbane audience, because the makers use two syllables.

Moving on to reds, more recently Pinot Noir (think the movie *Sideways*) gave way to Merlot, which is giving way to

Malbec. I remain partial to a Cab or a nice Chianti. I could do an entire post just on changing tastes in wine.

Back to what to order when you go out to eat. When I worked in midtown Manhattan, one of my go-to lunches at the Brasserie on East 53rd was steak tartare. It's gone (the tartare, not the Brasserie), and not just because of Mad Cow disease. Blood red meat is considered too *Mad Men* macho; it's also bad for your cholesterol. Everyone is more health conscious now. You're more likely to see tuna tartare than the beef version.

Sweetbreads and Rocky Mountain (or prairie) oysters seem to have disappeared, too. What's that about? Did the Internet make it easier for people to find out what they were actually eating? And frogs' legs. Several species of frogs are endangered. Have we finally grown a social conscience? More likely it's because France enacted laws to protect them in 1980. I doubt that Julia Child would include *Cuisses de Grenouille* in a new edition of *Mastering the Art of French Cooking*.

Many of my more salient food memories have been tossed into the gastronomic InSinkErator. It should make me angry, but it just makes me sad. I guess I should thank the Lord for small favors. All the items that are on Luke's increasingly short list of acceptable foods are still available in supermarkets. There are some things he just won't eat. He'll sniff them, give them a poke or two and then walk away. That's probably what Jagdish would do if I served him Greek yoghurt. Let's hope we never have to find out.

Retiree's Life in Pie Charts

Original Post Date Jun. 29, 2013

This chapter is a visual one: viewing a typical retiree's life in pie charts. Special thanks to my Fly Fox friend for suggesting this idea. The legends with percentages are repeated below the charts. They read clockwise, starting at 12 o'clock.

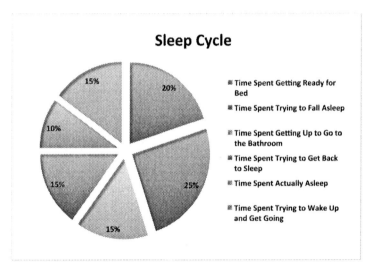

Sleep Cycle	%
Time Spent Getting Ready for Bed	20
Time Spent Trying to Fall Asleep	30
Time Spent Getting Up to Go to the Bathroom	5
Time Spent Trying to Get Back to Sleep	15
Time Spent Actually Asleep	15
Time Spent Trying to Wake Up and Get Going	15

Doctors' Appointments

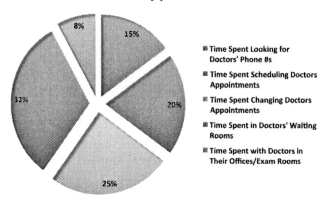

- Time Spent Looking for Doctors' Phone #s
- Time Spent Scheduling Doctors Appointments
- Time Spent Changing Doctors Appointments
- Time Spent in Doctors' Waiting Rooms
- Time Spent with Doctors in Their Offices/Exam Rooms

Doctors' Appointments	%
Time Spent Looking for Doctors' Phone #s	15
Time Spent Scheduling Doctors Appointments	20
Time Spent Changing Doctors Appointments	25
Time Spent in Doctors' Waiting Rooms	32
Time Spent w/Doctors in Their Offices/Exam Rms	8

Food Cycle

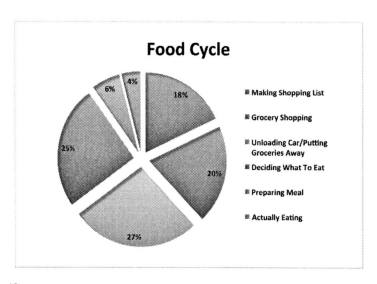

- Making Shopping List
- Grocery Shopping
- Unloading Car/Putting Groceries Away
- Deciding What To Eat
- Preparing Meal
- Actually Eating

Food Cycle	%
Making Shopping List	18
Grocery Shopping	20
Unloading Car/Putting Groceries Away	27
Deciding What To Eat	25
Preparing Meal	6
Actually Eating	4

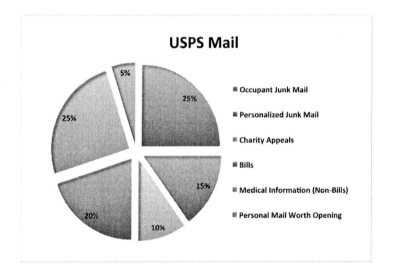

USPS Mail	%
Occupant Junk Mail	25
Personalized Junk Mail	15
Charity Appeals	10
Bills	20
Medical Information (Non-Bills)	25
Personal Mail Worth Opening	5

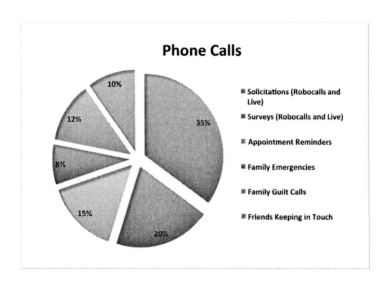

Phone Calls

- Solicitations (Robocalls and Live)
- Surveys (Robocalls and Live)
- Appointment Reminders
- Family Emergencies
- Family Guilt Calls
- Friends Keeping in Touch

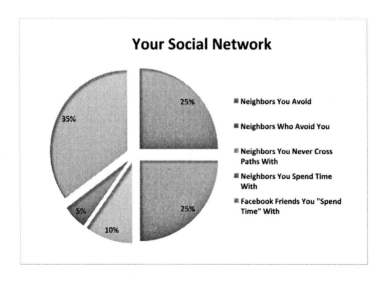

Your Social Network

- Neighbors You Avoid
- Neighbors Who Avoid You
- Neighbors You Never Cross Paths With
- Neighbors You Spend Time With
- Facebook Friends You "Spend Time" With

Phone Calls	%
Solicitations (Robocalls and Live)	35
Surveys (Robocalls and Live)	20
Appointment Reminders	15
Family Emergencies	8
Family Guilt Calls	12
Friends Keeping in Touch	10

Your Social Network	%
Neighbors You Avoid	25
Neighbors Who Avoid You	25
Neighbors You Never Cross Paths With	10
Neighbors You Spend Time With	5
Facebook Friends You "Spend Time" With	35

There you have it. A typical retiree's life, explained in easy to understand pie charts.

You (Insert Appropriate Phrase Here) for Your Age

Original Post Date Aug. 24, 2013

Have you noticed how often someone pays you a half-baked compliment these days by ending whatever it is with "for your age"? (Or some equally dismissive qualifier.) A head nod to my friend Keith Mosher for suggesting this blog topic for *Retirement Sparks*. I knew the minute he said it that he had a great idea—for someone his age.

"You're really quite agile!" sounds like a vote of approval for how you avoided being mowed down by a fully-loaded, runaway shopping cart in a parking lot. That is, until the person who lost control of the cart adds: "for someone your age." Lucky for them you're agile, because we're also litigious at our age.

"You smell lovely!" brings a smile to your face and lifts your spirits. But then you hear the after-remark: "for an old lady." That's when you shoot back: "And you don't smell half bad either, for an old fart." Speaking of which, why is it everyone seems to think that people over 65 are out-of-control fart machines? If we pass a ripe one, it's usually because we really meant to, as a sort of olfactory editorial.

Then there's the brain-function comments. "You sure seem to have your wits about you." "You're pretty sharp!" "You catch on quickly." All for—you guessed it—someone my age. It's inevitable that the brainpower of seniors will provoke remarks. What can we expect when we tote around books of Sudoku and crossword puzzles? Some of us do it to fight off senility. Others use them to kill time in doctors' waiting rooms. Maybe we should wrap them in brown paper bags. Or the recycled cover of *Fifty Shades of Grey*.

The most offensive comment is: "You're really interesting to talk to, for someone your age." This remark is always delivered with a look of utter amazement. Do they really think that the only things people over 65 talk about are their medications and their digestive systems? We read the paper (perhaps more often in a printed version than they do, but we read it). We keep up on current events and political issues. How else would we know how much better life was when we were younger?

Sometimes I'm tempted to reply: "And you're surprisingly literate and well-informed for someone so young!" But really, what's the point? They probably haven't got a clue about sarcasm.

For most of my adult life, I didn't wear a lot of makeup. When I painted my face for some special event, colleagues would often tell me: "You clean up nice." Now when I hear this, it's usually followed by one of those odious age-qualifiers. I'd like to think I'd still clean up nice even if I weren't of a certain age. Hope springs eternal.

One thing I'm aware of whenever I'm out is keeping my spine erect, whether I'm walking or sitting. I'm convinced that decent posture is one way to confuse people about how old I really am. I base this on the fact that the elderly are expected to be hunched over, bent over, doubled over or just plain folded over. I know I'm losing this battle when I hear that I have nice posture for my age. That's enough to make me sit with my head between my knees.

I've always walked at a good clip, for two reasons. One is that I'm short, so I need to take three steps for every two that the person next to me takes. That makes we walk briskly. Also, I worked in Manhattan for 20 years. If you lollygag there, you're a prime target for purse snatchers and muggers. When you walk fast, they figure you're a native and you don't suffer fools gladly. They move on to the meanderers. These days my brisk walk is likely to generate one of those "for your age" comments.

No. I don't walk fast "for my age." I walk fast for my height. Or for someone my weight. Or for a person who has absolutely no place to be this afternoon and all the time in the world to get there. And don't you forget it, even if you do have a terrible memory—for someone your age. (Insert sarcasm font here.)

Modern Deadly Sins

Original Post Date Aug. 31, 2013

Someone posted a photo of brightly colored wristbands on Facebook. At first glance, they looked like the charity bands you see: yellow Live Strong, pink Komen Breast Cancer, red AIDS awareness. On closer inspection, they had the names of the seven deadly sins etched into them. My friend was wearing Lust, Sloth and Gluttony. My first thought was: there should be one that reads "Facebooking," which in turn led to this post.

Just as the Seven Wonders of the Ancient World were updated to the Seven Wonders of the Modern World, we should have Ten Modern Deadly Sins. There will be more than seven, because from a retiree's perspective, many things should send people straight to hell today. I give them to you here, starting, of course, with *Facebooking*.

Facebooking *per se* is not a deadly sin, but *Obsessive Facebooking* is, and many Facebookers are obsessive about it. Deadly sins are often about excess, and FB can be addictive, which leads to damnable excess. Some of my FB friends post so many tidbits that it takes hours to scroll through my news feed. Since these morsels can often be interesting or funny or informative, I'm afraid to skip over them. Go ahead, charge me with FOMO (Fear Of Missing Out), but please don't do it on my Facebook news feed.

People who are obsessed with FB are sometimes also guilty of the deadly sin of *Emoticonstipation*. This occurs when you over-stuff electronic messages with emoticons (those yellow smiley faces and such). My niece, Pam, has cleverly suggested that Textlax might cure someone of this behavior. If you're going to use emoticons, at least download a variety of styles. Like the cartoon cats. Cats are never sinful.

The modern version of the original deadly sin Gluttony is *Gluteny*, which emerged from the explosive growth of folks following gluten-free diets. Not everyone who avoids gluten is guilty of Gluteny. The ones bound for hell are those who insist on gluten-free food even when they're not gluten-intolerant. They drive everyone around them crazy just because they have a FOMO on this food trend.

Closely related to Gluteny is *Veganizing*. There are many good reasons why people become vegans. Bill Clinton did it because even after his bypass operation, his arteries were building up cholesterol. Being a vegan is not a sin. But trying to convert carnivores to vegans (especially without passing through a vegetarian phase) is a deadly no-no. Let people decide on their own to cut out red meat, cheese and everything tasty known to modern man.

I'll bet many will agree that *Apostrophornication* is one of the worst transgressions. People apostrophornicate when they misuse (or more likely, fail to use) apostrophes. The two most common examples are using "your" instead of "you're" and "there" (or "their") instead of "they're". This makes those who respect punctuation and grammar very angry. Since anger is an original deadly sin, that one gets charged to the 'phornicator, too.

Speaking of grammar, *Substitupidity* (the use of "I" instead of "me," "she" instead of "her," etc.) is also a cardinal offense. I'm especially irked when I hear a newscaster commit it. It's bad enough when local media personalities do this; they're— notice correct use of apostrophe here—lower down in the network food chain. But national talking heads are frequently guilty, as well. "Send Tom and I a message on FB." On second thought, don't.

A truly modern deadly sin is *Moblastphemy*—talking loudly on a mobile phone in public. It's deadly no matter where you do it, but if it's in a restaurant or a theater, you should go straight to hell, IMHO (In My Humble Opinion).

We must also list *Peeping Thongery*—it's as deadly as they come. No explanation needed, but it's especially lethal for women of a certain age. In the interest of gender-fairness, let's include *Plumbersbuttitis*. Both sexes can be guilty of each of these, but we see Thongery mostly in women and Buttitis in men. In medicine, "-itis" signals the inflammation of something. Plumbers' butts always look fatter than average, and they inflame our gag reflex. Enough said.

Finally, we have the newest modern deadly sin: *Air Humping*, a combination of two news items. Chicago Mayor Rahm Emanuel was videotaped "chair humping" the back of a folding chair at the Taste of Chicago event. Singer Miley Cyrus (in an effort to leave Hannah Montana in her rearview) burned "twerking" into the media mainstream with her gyrations on the VMA show (MTV Video Music Awards). Gag and double gag.

These visuals sent me straight to my stash of *vino*. Fortunately, moderate imbibing is not on the list of deadly sins, original or modern. Praise the Lord and pass the chianti.

Post-FRA Acronyms

Original Post Date Nov. 16, 2013

Some months before I retired and almost a year before I reached Full Retirement Age (FRA), I wrote a blog post about the acronyms for retirement jargon, including FRA. It turns out that post-FRA there are new acronyms I need to deal with.

Last week I had my mid-year checkup. I was feeling pretty good about it. I'd lost 28 pounds from my visit six months earlier and my blood pressure (BP) was down to 120 over 80. It had crept up to the 140 over 90 range before I lost the weight. Then I noticed the column on the report of my visit headed "Conditions" and saw that I'm still overweight. Well (thought I), at least it doesn't say "obese."

My goal had been to lose another 10 pounds, maybe 15. I decided to go on-line to find out where I need to be so that I'm no longer overweight. I've reached the age where I've been shrinking a bit each year, and I was prepared for my target weight to shrink along with my height. Shrink, yes, but wither to something not realistically attainable, no. There are tons of websites that claim to help you calculate your ideal body weight.

You have *healthstatus.com* and *healthcentral.com*. There's *healthdiscovery.net* and *healthchecksystems.com*. Also the basic *calculator.net* and the ever-popular *webmd.com*. Some of the sites require you to input your body frame (small-boned, average, large-boned). To do this accurately, you're supposed to use calipers and measure your elbow thickness, or else try to wrap your fingers around your wrist. I took the easy way out and went with average frame.

On that basis, some of the sites still label me obese. They all claim that I need to lose at least 25 additional pounds to reach normal weight for my current height. What's worse, one site actually had the temerity to tell me that I can consume just 896 calories a day if I want to lose weight. As if! I lost the 28 pounds eating 1100-1200. Did I say "eating?" I meant "starving."

The culprit in these calculations is the BMI (Body Mass Index). That acronym was not unfamiliar to me, but I had paid it little mind, and I certainly didn't know how to calculate it. For those who care: divide your body weight in pounds by your height in inches squared. Then multiply that times 703. A normal BMI is 19 to 24.9, give or take a pinch, depending on the website.

I used to joke that no husband should be allowed to weigh less than his wife. My husband is extremely thin, so despite my extra baggage, I always felt he was partly to blame for the disconnect in our poundage. Now I see that it's all my fault. When I reach my proper weight—notice I say when, not if— I will finally weigh less than he does.

By the end of the week, the euphoria of my official weight loss and improved BP had morphed into the depressing realization that it could be six more months before I can resume visiting my wine rack once a week. You would think I would have left well enough alone and settled in with a good book. You would be wrong. I returned to the Internet to do research on yet another post-FRA acronym: RMD.

I will turn 69 next year and that has put RMD (Required Minimum Distribution) on my radar. It's the amount one must withdraw from one's IRA after age 70 1/2. Well, not exactly. According to a variety of websites (including Uncle Sam's), you have to start withdrawing the money by April 1 of the calendar year *after* the year in which you turn 70 1/2 (*not* 70). I determined that to be April 1, 2017 for me. How much one has to withdraw turns out to be not so straight-forward either.

The government's Uniform Lifetime Table (ULT) calculates your Life Expectancy Factor (LEF). It plugs that into a chart to show the percentage of your IRA you have to withdraw. Each year longer that you live, your projected longevity gets extended, so the percentage changes every year. In other words, you can't just sit down when you hit 70 1/2 and figure out how much to take out for each of the next five years, calculate the taxes you'll owe and determine how much you'll have left to buy really fine wine.

If I had not known how high my BMI is, the RMD based on the LEF in the ULT would have driven me straight into the arms of a *Montepulciano d'Abruzzo* to lower my BP. Instead I find myself in front of an open refrigerator, communing with a jar of baby dill pickles (5 calories each). It's a cruel world.

Banned Words for 2014

Original Post Date Jan. 4, 2014

January is the time for the annual lists of banned words and phrases. This marks the third year that I've been publishing my own compendium. I put my list together in mid-November, and it turns out my first three entries also top the annual list just released by Michigan's Lake Superior State University. Their order is different, but we agree on the three words we'd most like to hear less (or none) of in 2014.

Number one on my list may surprise you. I don't want to hear '**hashtag**' anymore. I'm content to have people use hashtags. I don't even mind seeing the # symbol. I'm just weary of hearing the word. We'll need something to replace it when we speak, so I've created a substitute. Since the hashtag has historically been referred to as the number sign, let's call it the NuSi. It should take a few years before that gets annoying enough to show up in my annual post.

'**Selfie**' is next. Oxford Dictionaries declared it the 2013 "Word of the Year" because of its meteoric rise in use, but that doesn't mean we have to like it. I'd be happy if we not only stopped using it, but we also stopped taking them. I know: not gonna happen, but a girl can dream. And BTW (by the way), my list was created before the Pope and Obama posed for their infamous year-end selfies.

Close behind, and no surprise, are 'twerk' and 'twerking.' (These count as one entry, for those keeping track.) As with selfie, my hope is that people not only stop saying this, they also stop doing it. I have only a slightly better chance of that happening than I do seeing an end to the photo behavior. With twerking, some equally repulsive move could replace it in 2014. (Remember: 'Gangnam Style' was on last year's list.)

Can we also do without 'bromance'? It may be popular in some circles, but I never hear anyone singing: "A fine bromance, with no kisses; A fine bromance, my friend, this is." That's likely due to the unstated understanding that a bromance never involves kisses. Frankly, I'm not sure what it does or doesn't involve, other than being annoying. A guy can appreciate the qualities and appeal of another guy without needing to slap a label on what he thinks or feels. Oorah!

In the interest of equal time for the opposite sex, let's also do away with 'bestie,' the latest patois for 'best friend.' It alternates with BFF (Best Friends Forever), but BFF doesn't make that nails-on-the-blackboard sound that bestie does. Besides, bestie originated as slang from the Brits. Not an export they're likely proud of. It's probably barely ahead of Marmite and haggis.

Moving on to politically-based candidates (words and phrases, that is), 'Tea Party' (the label, not the political perspective) has no place in Congress. I'm fine with 'conservative' and 'libertarian,' but 'Tea Party' has become far too polarizing. Let the Mad Hatters fend for themselves as individuals who hold strong beliefs, or as members of more traditional coalitions. But fie on letting them find shelter using the Tea Party label. It's become an anathema even to most Republicans.

As we say goodbye to Tea Party, let's also say ta-ta to '**brinksmanship**.' Use it, and I'll tune out before the third syllable rolls off your tongue. I'm tossing it onto the lexicographic dust heap, along with '**hostage**.' These words (and concepts) have no place in Congress. If we have to ban them to get our elected officials to stop engaging in this behavior and to have the Media stop celebrating it, so be it.

I'm also so over '**fumble**,' as in 'fumble the rollout' or 'fumble the ball.' What happened with the Affordable Care Act (aka Obamacare) was so beyond a fumble that we need to call it something else. How about a disaster?

Speaking of disasters, I'd really like to not hear '**natural disaster**' anymore. Note to God: please don't send us any in 2014, so we won't need to use this phrase. That's probably too much to expect. I have no suggestions for what else to call these when they happen, but I wanted to include this phrase on principle and in a spirit of optimism.

Okay, let's not count 'natural disaster' among my ten. That means I need one more. Let's give up the phrase '**turn the page**.' That's pretty much what a lot of politicians are hoping we'll do in 2014, but let's not memorialize it in words. As Nike says, let's "just do it."

Those are my ten candidates that should not be uttered in mixed company in 2014. By mixed company, I mean by anyone else when I'm in the room.

Fear of Balding

Original Post Date Feb. 1, 2014

Through most of my life, the physical feature in which I took the most pride was my hair. OK. Maybe that alternated with my eyes, which are so dark a brown they're almost black. But I had no control over my eyes. My hair, on the other hand, I could cut short, grow long, style up or leave down. All of which I did over time. And did again.

The company where I worked for 17 years purchased doll bodies during the holidays for needy children. Employees dressed them and handmade outfits competed for prizes. Winners were photographed, giving me a visual history of my changing styles, from updos and hair so long I could sit on it, to short, professional cuts that look almost androgynous.

Shortly after I left the company, I was diagnosed with stage two breast cancer. Chemotherapy left me temporarily bald. Surprisingly, this did not distress me. Perhaps that was because I had the (probably mistaken) notion that I looked cute bald. Or exotic or artsy or just interesting. This was around the time the duck-fuzzed Sinead O'Connor was in her heyday.

In my book, *Cancer: A Coping Guide*, I recount the story of my mother's reaction to seeing me bald.

Once, when I visited my mother and had my head covered with a scarf, I could tell that she was curious to see what my bald head looked like underneath. I told her I'd show her, if she promised not to cry when she saw it. She said she wouldn't. As soon as I took off the scarf, her mouth started to crinkle up. "Here come the waterworks," I thought. But instead, she burst into a fit of uncontrollable laughter.

When my hair grew back in, I kept it long for awhile. My mother nagged me to cut it short. She may have laughed at my bald head, but she never liked the way I looked with long tresses. I reminded her that I was forced to go without hair for over a year. I just wanted to be able to run my fingers through it and really brush it for a change.

Eventually, I tired of long styles again and had it cut. My mother was right, of course. I do look better with it short. It's been at least a dozen years since I've had locks down to my shoulders or longer. Let's face it: older women look better with shorter dos. Most of them dye their hair lighter, hoping the color will blend with their increasingly visible scalp.

One reason my hair was special was that I had extremely thick tresses. I followed the daily toilette prescribed by my Madison Avenue stylist, George Michael. (He serviced one style only: long and straight.) His directive: lean forward, head down, and brush from the nape to the ends 100 times every day, using a natural bristle brush. I kept doing this even with short dos until around the time I retired. Then I got lazy.

Whether a consequence of my laziness, or an inevitable aspect of aging, I can't say. But my hair has become finer and less populous. I worry that I'm going bald. The strays left in the shower drain when I wash my locks are forming ever-larger clumps. There is no pouf left in my crown. Every morning, the mirror reveals a demoralizing reflection of "bed hair" or "pillow head" or whatever you choose to call that look that says: "I didn't bother to brush it or comb it. What's the point? It has a mind of its own."

In the winter, there's also static electricity. Thin wisps rise up in drafts of heated air, leaving me looking like a psychotic Alfalfa from Our Gang. If I dampen them to kill the static, my hair flattens and I look even more like I'm balding. All year long, I find strands on my clothes. Occasionally, it's a really long one that has somehow remained embedded in the loops of an old sweater, reminding me of how my crown jewel used to look. Mostly, they just remind me that they're falling out.

I cannot ignore it any longer. I am going bald. And at a rapidly increasing pace. Perhaps if I return to that daily ritual of brushing 100 times, I can slow the process. I wonder what my mother would think about this. She'd probably tell me to dye my hair light and get a perm. (She thought that curls hid her bald spot.) Somewhere up there, George Michael is having a coronary. I can almost hear him shouting: "97, 98, 99, 100!"

Aging's Real "Tell"
Original Post Date May 10, 2014

My girlhood friends and I looked forward to the summer carnivals in a nearby town, especially the man who guessed your age. Like many girls in their teens, we wanted to appear older. The man always pegged us to within a year (the agreed upon window for him to be correct). I couldn't understand how he got it right. Looking back, I suppose it was easy. A group of giggling girls had to be about the same age. He probably scanned our faces, threw out the high and low estimates and went with the average.

Now at the opposite end of the age scale, I prefer to be gauged younger than I am. The older I get, the less often that happens. At first, I blamed this on my graying hair, so I started dying the roots. That helped for a few years, but gradually, the knowing looks and the polite "ma'ams" started again.

At that point, I assumed it was those stubborn age spots on my face and the backs of my hands. I tried using Porcelana cream for awhile. After a few months with minimal fading, I lost interest (and patience) and used some makeup concealer instead.

As I applied the cream to my hands, I realized that my knuckles were getting that craggy look that comes with the advent of arthritis. A sure sign of aging. I remember someone telling me that the hands were one of the ways the carnival age-guessers pegged the older women.

Then there was the pooch under my neck. As I aged, I gained weight. With the weight came more of a pooch. A pooch in and of itself doesn't make you look old. What's left behind when you lose that weight does. Now that I've shed 35 pounds since last year's shock-inducing physical, my neck pooch has turned into an out-and-out wattle. Wattles make you look old. They need to be covered with things like turtlenecks and scarves. Or necklaces with fat beads. Or multiple strands. Or multiple strands of fat beads.

As I took inventory of these signs of aging over the years, I thought I had accounted for everything that would give away my age. I didn't have a plan for hiding all those "tells," but I did a passable job of camouflaging most of them. I thought I had my appearance under control. Until a few weekends ago.

Sunday mornings are the time we lollygag around the bedroom for awhile before we head down to watch the political talk shows. For those who are snickering, "lollygag" is not a code word for sex. I'm using it as the around-the-house equivalent of puttering in the garage or workshop.

One recent Sunday, my lollygagging led me to clip my toenails. That's when the real "tell" about old age hit me. I always had cute feet; small feet; delicate feet. The beginnings of a bunion, perhaps, but not that prominent. My arches were pronounced from years of wearing high heels in Manhattan on my walk from the Port Authority to Park and 50th and back every day. But that just made them look cuter.

I need to take a step backward for a moment and tell you about what happened to my mother as she got older. She visited a podiatrist every few months to have her toenails clipped. I thought it was because she wasn't limber enough to clip them herself. To that end, I do stretching exercises every morning, making sure my toes stay well within reach. But without my reading glasses, they're just a blur down there.

When I put on my glasses that Sunday the better to clip my nails, I was stunned by what I saw. My feet are not cute anymore. I now have old feet and ugly-ass toenails. I recognized them almost immediately. They're my mother's toenails, the ones that forced her to prevail upon a podiatrist for pedicures. Perhaps the reason she made those trips wasn't because she couldn't reach her toes. Perhaps it was because she couldn't bear to look at her nails close up.

There it is. The hard, bitter truth. The real "tell" of aging isn't gray hair. It isn't age spots. It's not wrinkled knuckles or a neck wattle. It's those ugly-ass toenails and I have them.

Loss of Padding

Original Post Date Nov. 8, 2014

My husband left for India on Tuesday. He'll be gone about three weeks. This presents a welcome opportunity for me to attack a major project. Since I'd like to get my next edition of *Retirement Sparks* to print before yearend, I can use this window of uninterrupted time to assemble the book for publication. I had started on this last spring but had to shift gears to prep the house for sale once again.

After three days of sitting at my computer for hours at a time this week, I had one of those Aha! (Oh, no!) moments. My fanny was killing me. My lower back wasn't exactly thrilled with me either, but the pain in my butt was something new. Those who have never met me in person, especially before I lost 30 pounds last year, might not see this as an Aha! moment. So, here's some back(side) story.

I've always had a lot of "junk in the trunk." My sister, my brother and I all inherited my father's behind. (Our mother's rear end was as flat as a pancake.) Because I fenced in high school, my *gluteus maximus* was especially well-developed. And it didn't bounce around. It stayed that way even after college, probably because I walked briskly and a lot when I worked in Manhattan. And usually in high heels. (Lots of muscle flexing…)

I considered my derrière an asset, since men seemed to like big butts, even before Sir Mix-a-Lot came out with his song, *Baby Got Back*. ("I like big butts and I cannot lie...") By the way, if you haven't seen Jimmy Fallon's remix of Brian Williams rapping to that song, you must check it out on YouTube.

Returning to this week's painful realization: my bottom has lost much of its cushioning capability. Though some of this is probably due to my weight loss, it's more likely another sad side effect of growing old. I say this because I had already noticed that the balls of my feet were no longer doing a good job of making walking comfortable either. Simply put: my body is losing padding.

No one tells you to expect this. Fallen arches, yes. But you don't hear folks saying: "You'll feel like you're walking on concrete unless you wear special shoes." And you certainly don't have folks warning you that at some point, you're going to think you're sitting directly on your ass bone. (*Is* there an ass bone? I know it wouldn't be the tailbone. That's in the middle, at the base of the spine.) Moving on...

I suppose I wouldn't be as miffed at this loss of padding in useful places if it weren't that I've been gaining it in places I don't need it. Or want it. Take for instance my belly. No, really. Please take the extra padding I have there. (Thank you, Rodney Dangerfield.) Despite the collateral tummy tuck that came along with one of my cancer surgeries, I was left with plenty of space for fat cells to proliferate. And proliferate they did.

Scientists should research a method of shifting belly fat to the fanny area. That ought to be pretty easy. They already do liposuction after all. Just reposition the stuffing laterally about 180 degrees. If someone can figure out a way to do that, they'll make a fortune. People our age won't even care if it leaves some scars.

Of course, there's also the extra cushioning on our upper arms. Actually, I'm not sure it's accurate to call it cushioning if it dangles. Whatever. It's padding I don't need, don't want, and can't seem to get rid of. If those same scientists can take that upper arm flab and reposition it to the bottoms of our feet, they'll have something irresistible to peddle in the AARP publications.

Did I mention my neck wattle yet? Maybe not in today's post, but you've certainly read plenty about it during the years that I've been blogging. There's not enough excess there to help with my feet, but I'd still like to get rid of it. Just sayin'.

Seriously, how many of you had given any thought to this problem as part of your adjustment to retirement? I'm warning you: put this on your radar now. Start looking for extra-thick gel inserts for your shoes and a Kardashian butt enhancer today. I cannot lie. You'll thank me later.

Retirement Sparks Redux

Section III

Retirement Updates and Issues

Save the Penny
Original Post Date Feb. 2, 2014; rev. Oct. 2014

Be still my heart. There's a proposal afoot to get rid of the penny. Speaking of a foot, the first thought that came to my mind when I heard this was: *"Where would that leave penny loafers?"* I suppose they'd have to become dime loafers; a nickel wouldn't fit in the slot. Besides, at least one economist is advocating that the government also stop minting the nickel.

"Why?" (You may be wondering.) Simple economics. A September 2014 issue of *Time* magazine reported that the U.S. mint lost $55 million in 2013 making pennies. It now costs 1.83 cents to make a penny (which contains mostly zinc today, not copper). The nickel costs ten cents to produce, so it's hardly a cost-effective substitute for the penny. That's why some folks feel it makes sense to kill two coins at the same time. And since we're talking twos, two days after I first looked into this, Canada discontinued its penny. The U.S. is watching what happens up north, but we'll probably ignore it.

The plans to jettison the penny generally propose rounding sales up or down to the nearest nickel. People are calling it a 'rounding tax,' since so many prices end in 99 cents. If we also drop the nickel, we'll need to round up or down to the nearest dime. If the potential financial costs to consumers aren't enough disin*cent*ive for these proposals, here are some emotional ones to consider if we remove *'penny'* from our collective conscience.

Getting rid of the penny would be the death knell for the *penny ante*. Not to get too maudlin here, but I still have the tin full of pennies that my late mother used when she played poker with her lady friends. The last member of her card group died last year at age 103.

The title (and lyrics) of the Beatles' song *Penny Lane* would have to be changed. Somehow *Two-Bit Alley* just doesn't have the same ring to it.

The expression: *"I'm like a bad penny; I keep turning up"* would lose its meaning. There would be no good pennies, and pennies in general would no longer keep turning up. I'm not sure how we'd replace this, but: *"I'm like a discontinued penny; I keep rounding up"* comes to mind.

Then there's the adage: *"A penny saved is a penny earned."* Not true. A penny saved would be a penny wasted. You'd need to turn them in at a bank to get anything for them, and eventually even Uncle Sam wouldn't want them.

How about the question: *"A penny for your thoughts?"* Would that become *"A silver dollar for your thoughts?"* It's bad enough the Tooth Fairy has suffered severe inflation over our lifetimes, but the Thought Inquirer? I shudder to think about it.

Continuing with thoughts and inflation, consider: *"For what it's worth, that's my two cents."* Turns out your two cents has actually been worth four cents, but what would it be worth now? A quarter? Or would you be dropping a dime?

Let's not forget *"penny-wise and pound-foolish."* Seems like a penny hasn't been wise for quite some time now, so perhaps we could just go with *"pound-wise and penny-foolish."* Of course, we're not Brits, so I guess we'd have to say *"dollar-wise and penny-foolish."*

How about your *Penny Valentine*? If you sent her roses on February 14, would she become your *Dime A Dozen Valentine*? Whatever you called her and whatever you sent her, what used to cost a *pretty penny* would now cost an arm and a leg.

Most other 'penny' expressions have survived out of nostalgia, so we could keep them. Penny postcards are long gone; eventually, postcards in general will be, too. Do you know what a two-cents plain is (or was)? Think soda fountains and the depression. Penny stocks have always been a euphemism and the penny arcade morphed into the video arcade over thirty years ago. One exception is *Pennysaver* newspapers; I'd like to see those be pro-active on this issue and become *Save-the-Penny* papers.

My favorite of all these expressions is one that I hadn't heard until I was getting fodder for this post. *"I felt like a penny waiting for change."* It means you felt helpless or worthless. If the penny and the nickel were taken out of circulation, this phrase would become: *"I felt like a dime waiting for change."* I think we should keep "penny" for this one and make it more existential: *"I felt like a penny waiting for Godot."*

Or perhaps just: *"I felt like a penny waiting."* And waiting. And waiting. And nobody came.

Sniff. It's just too sad to contemplate. Sorry. I need to go get a tissue.

Acronyms Redux for Retirees

Original Post Date Mar. 16, 2013

As a lover of language, I like to keep up with the acronyms in our pop culture. I'm not referring here to the text abbreviations used primarily for Instant Messaging (IM) or Twitter. I'm talking about phrases used in daily conversation or mainstream media. Lately I've amused myself by rejiggering the words that make up some of the better-known acronyms, tweaking them into something especially appropriate for retirees.

Take for example the political term RINO. When I first heard it, I assumed it was spelled Rhino and referred to elected officials who had a thick hide. Turns out it stands for *Republicans In Name Only*. This acronym begs to be redefined as *Retirees In Name Only*. From what I've seen, it's more of a truism than a nickname, since many retirees poke their noses into other people's business as a way to fight boredom.

I'm guilty of this myself. If I'm in a store, I'm compelled to tidy the racks of clothing and tempted to remerchandise them while I'm at it. That's bad enough in and of itself, but then I have to find the owner or manager and lecture them on keeping their stock in order. If I've moved things around, I explain why the way I've displayed the goods is superior to what they'd done. I'm a RINO if ever there was one.

Another good example is the hot property YOLO. It stands for *You Only Live Once*. It has bored its way into pop lingo through the song "The Motto" and the promotion of that motto via a tattoo sported by tweenybopper heartthrob, Zac Efron. The Urban Dictionary defines it as *The dumbass's excuse for something stupid that they did.*

Wikipedia tells us it's a motto similar to *carpe diem*, suggesting people "should enjoy life, even if that entails taking risks." That certainly sounds like a motto someone my age could live by. But since the youth culture owns YOLO, I'm giving retirees a phrase that's equally appropriate, but highly unlikely to be co-opted by trendy actors.

Our new motto shall be YODO—*You Only Die Once*. Think about it. We can engage in all sorts of risky behavior and when we're called out on it by friends and family, being lectured to take care lest we get injured (or worse), we can holler out: *"YODO! Deal with it."* Who are they kidding? It only matters to them because they don't want to get stuck taking care of us if we get incapacitated doing something stupid. YODO, Baby, YODO.

Closely related to YODO is YOGOO—*You Only Grow Old Once*. Like YODO, YOGOO can be used to excuse a plethora of bad behavior. It's more versatile than YODO, since YOGOO behavior doesn't need to be risky, just offensive. It has the added benefit of sounding like something you'd call a person engaging in that type of activity.

Another term I uncovered—one that was new to me—is FOMO. It stands for *Fear Of Missing Out* and explains why people sit through poorly conceived movies, attend boring lectures and eat at restaurants that are popular but, well… lousy. They don't want to miss out on something fashionable that they don't appreciate but almost everyone else (for reasons unknown to anyone with a glimmer of intelligence or good taste) does.

The retirees' version of FOMO is FOCO: *Fear Of Checking Out.* The older we get, the more we worry that we're going to predecease our peers and, by extension, MO on good stuff. We wouldn't want to ride off into the sunset the week before Ferran Adrià announces he's decided to resurrect *el Bulli* within walking distance of our condo development. (Thank you, nephew Barry, for enabling me to sound so worldly.)

We also don't want to CO until we've done everything on our bucket list. If we haven't made that list yet (like yours truly), we're in a precarious position. We could CO at anytime and not MO on anything we'd officially hoped to do. This is a good reason to make your own bucket list now. It gives you an incentive to live in a way that will keep you from C-ing O prematurely.

There are many more acronyms we could delve into. You might want to create a parlor game out of this. As for me, I'm redirecting my attention to putting together *my* bucket list.

Item one: Make this a very long list.

Item two: Do everything on it before I CO.

OK. That's a good start. I'm ready for a break. And a nice glass of wine.

TGFI. *(Thank God For Imbibing!)*

Kale Frenzy Hits Retirees

Original Post Date Mar. 22, 2013

Unless you've been living under a rock, you must be aware of the latest culinary craze. I'm talking about the kale frenzy. Everywhere you turn, kale is on the menu, in the grocery cart, on the plate or in the news. Once a lowly garnish, it's now a main ingredient. As a follower of pop culture, I wanted to learn more about this bitter vegetable.

My search turned up all sorts of claims for this so-called miracle green that has been around for thousands of years. It can prevent cancer! It can lower your cholesterol! It will help you lose weight! Kale cigarettes relieve stress (and they're legal)! If you plant it in decorative pots near your front door, your house will sell above the asking price! Enough of these outrageous claims. What does botany tell us this wonder food can offer retirees?

It's a member of the *Brassicacae* family—also known as *cruciferous* vegetables—which includes broccoli, Brussels sprouts, cabbage and cauliflower, among others. Its genus is *brassica*. I can see by your glazed-over eyes that this is TMI, so I won't go into its species. (Remember the taxonomy mnemonic: *King Phillip Came Over For Good Soup.*)

Kale's soar into the stratosphere of culinary popularity is likely due to the spate of spinach recalls that began in 2006, when a number of deaths and dozens of severe illnesses were traced to tainted shipments. Spinach recalls have become annual events, with the leafy green being cited for *e. coli* or *salmonella* contamination virtually every year from 2006 thru 2013, and at the end of that year, the death knell sounded for baby spinach.

At some point, a thinking person has to give up on spinach. It was a major contributor to my weight gain when that key ingredient in the pseudo-quiche was nowhere to be found, leading me to give up on the South Beach Diet. Now I'll try substituting kale, if I can locate the recipe. My stager cleared off my kitchen counters when we listed the house for sale, and the cookbooks wound up in a box somewhere in the basement.

Kale is touted on numerous websites where health information and recipes abound. *WebMD.com* calls it a "nutritional powerhouse." The site tells us a cup of kale has 5 grams of fiber and contains more than 100% of the RDAs for the anti-oxidant vitamins A, C, and K. It's also a good source of calcium, B6, magnesium and lutein (for eye health). All that in just 36 calories, presuming you steam it or eat it raw. Sauce it and all bets are off.

Now that we're experts on the virtues of kale, let's talk about what to do with it. Use it raw, steamed, braised, pickled or baked. Eat it on its own (salads); use it as an additive (soups or pastas) or a topping (pizza); chop and bake it into something less predictable (chips).

In the *SunTimes.com*, Leah Zeldes described kale as "the new bacon," which sounds a tad extreme to me. I trust she did research to substantiate her report that "*Bon Appetit* named a kale salad its 2012 dish of the year," and that the green stuff "stars in some 43,000 YouTube videos." I'm not anal retentive enough to search YouTube to confirm her count.

The *Baltimore Sun* recipe for kale with pappardelle and sun-dried tomatoes sounds (and looks) yummy. (Thank you, John Houser III.) I've put kale and pine nuts on my shopping list, since many sites combine those ingredients in pastas, salads or snacks—all staples of retirees' diets.

I have some ideas for using kale that haven't made their way onto the Internet—yet. For example, mush the leaves into a gritty paste. Then use it to clean dentures. Or, in a nod to St. Patrick, add it to pale ale to make green beer. I'll be testing ground kale as an insect repellent around my tomatoes. Likewise to deter the slugs that dine on my petunia blossoms in the dead of night. And the caterpillars that chow down on them in broad daylight.

It's clear to me that kale will continue its rise as a darling of American cuisine. I'm going out on a limb to predict some consequences of this infatuation. Within three years, a celebrity will name her baby boy Kale. Seven years later, there will be five kids named Kale in every first grade class, and two of them will be girls. None of the kids will be named Spinach or Bacon. Bets anyone?

Amusement Park Rides
for Retirees
Original Post Date Jun. 1, 2013

When Summer is almost upon us, TV is replete with soft news about the latest amusement park rides, or classic rides that are being refurbished. We don't hear much about amusement park rides that have been designed (or redesigned) especially for retirees. Good news. I'm addressing that in today's post.

I grew up in a lake community that was about a half hour from a quaint amusement park called Bertrand's Island. Several times each summer, a handful of chaperones took a bus full of kids there on Nickel Night. Just as it sounds, every ride cost only a nickel, except the wooden roller coaster, and that was a dime. The line for the coaster was always long, but once on it, you could pay another dime and stay for another run. I once rode the coaster 26 times straight and it wasn't even on a dare.

Back in my heyday, one of the favorite rides of teenagers with raging hormones was the Tunnel of Love (aka Fun in the Dark). You cuddled in a little boat that drifted through dark, winding waterways that eventually whooshed you back to the dock where you began. The ride never lasted long enough. Retirees are welcomed to the *Tunnel of Vision*, where the boat hustles you through a tunnel that is pitch black on all sides. A blinding light in the middle leads the way out, and you can't get there soon enough.

One ride I never understood until I started working full time and needed to release some aggression was the bumper cars. Predictably, these have been replaced with *Bumper Scooters*. If you thought bumper cars were an extreme sport, wait until you've taken a spin on Bumper Scooters. The seniors who drive them are so vicious that you need to wear helmets and sign a hold-harmless agreement to go on this ride.

Young girls were especially susceptible to the Fortune Teller's charms. We knew it was hogwash, but who cared? As long as we were told we'd find true love and live happily ever after. Female retirees are more likely to be lured into the web of the *Misfortune Teller*. She'll predict all the physical ailments that are going to befall you and members of your family. Tip her generously and she just may inform you that her "crystal ball" (read: smart phone) malfunctioned. *WebMD* is now telling her things won't be that bad for you after all.

Not every amusement park had a Lost Continent ride, but every park for retirees has a *Lost Continence*. This is not so much a ride as an attraction. It's a centrally located area with private booths where you can refresh your adult underwear. Vending machines are conveniently positioned inside the doorway. Can't find it on the park map? It's near the *Lost Memory* station, right next to the *Lost Eyeglasses* booth.

One of my favorite rides was The Whip. I remember once trying to talk my friend into going on it with me. The only way I could convince her was by paying her fare as well as my own. She was, as we say, "a big girl," and unfortunately, I sat on the wrong side of her. When the Whip got going full bore, centrifugal force pushed her entire weight on top of me. I had to pull myself out from under her, fighting the force, to get to the uphill side. The retirees' version of this ride is *The Whiplash*. Enough said.

No amusement park worth its salt would be without a Ferris Wheel, and the retirees' park is no exception. While most wheels today are built taller and taller (think the Millennium Wheel in London, or the Dubai Eye), the one for us seniors suffers from the same height and movement challenges as we do. Every year the *Ferris Wheelchair* gets a little bit shorter and moves a tad slower. When last I checked, it stood just thirty feet tall, had six chairs on it and took twenty minutes to make one full rotation.

One ride that mercifully has changed very little since our youth is the Carousel. Sometimes now called the *Horseless Carousel*, the only difference is that there are no animals that go up and down and give us vertigo. Or more accurately: exacerbate our already-existing vertigo. The ride now has just those beautifully painted chariots with tufted leather seats, but you can still reach for that brass ring.

Ah, yes. Nothing says Summer like a trip to the local amusement park. And I don't mean those Six Flags extravaganzas. I'm talking about the ones with a manageable number of relatively simple rides and attractions. And especially ones designed with retirees in mind. Ticket, please.

Bamboo Is the New Flax

Original Post Date Jul. 27, 2013

About twenty years ago, flax became extremely popular, especially compared to another natural fiber, hemp. Since you can't smoke flax, other uses had to be found for this plant. Flax became a leading fiber of choice for clothing, thanks largely to the eponymous brand. It also showed up in soft goods for the household and in other items of décor.

Now we're in a new millennium, a new century, and two decades beyond flax. I've discovered that bamboo is the new flax. I cannot believe what items are touted as being made from bamboo. I would expect to see it in housewares and décor—in things like baskets and placemats, and tiki lights and wind chimes. Can you believe there are companies selling sink backsplashes made from bamboo? Wouldn't they get mildewed when wet?

Worse, I think of bamboo as a product that is brittle and throws off splinters easily. That quality made me sit up and take notice at some of the products I uncovered. Cutting boards and salad bowls, while not totally outrageous on their face, would have me worried about using ones made from bamboo. If I find fiber in my salad, I want to have put it there.

What really stopped me dead in my mental tracks was an ad in a Tuesday Morning flier for bamboo sheets. Yes, sheets.

Would you roll around on sheets made from a product that sheds sharp little pieces of itself? I don't care how fine the "thread count" is; I won't be buying bamboo bedding. No way. No how.

Bamboo is showing up outside of home goods, too. Some of those uses aren't surprising. Bamboo bicycles must be light and easy to pedal around town. Sunglasses and yoga mats don't seem like a stretch, though leggings might be. The names of some of the companies selling this stuff are noteworthy, too. There's Bambooki and Boo Bamboo and BumBoosa, for instance. (More on that last one later.)

Electronics accessories are a popular area of use: bamboo laptop cases, USB flash drives, PC keyboards and mice. Impecca makes a hand-carved designer bamboo mouse available in cherry, walnut, espresso or natural colors. SigniCASE offers 23 different iPhone cases in bamboo.

I can see that none of this has you itching and scratching. Well, how about this: bamboo hair and beauty products, like the Bamboo Charcoal Face & Body Soap Bar. Or a revitalizing hair conditioning treatment. Or products for eyelashes and eyebrows. I'm clumsy enough putting on mascara. I wouldn't want to worry about splinters in my eyes, too.

Still not skeeved out by any of these products? Here are my absolute favorite bamboo items you can now buy from BumBoosa. Diaper liners, baby wipes and toilet paper rolls (individually wrapped—zero plastic!) These are guaranteed bio-friendly products. The baby wipes are even award winning. Non-synthetic and "tree-free." Users of the TP describe it as "eco-luxurious." BumBoosa claims it's "processed using the thermo-mechanical pulping method." Who can resist whatever that is?

I'll tell you who: I can. I may be showing my own ignorance. Toilet paper comes from trees after all. Or maybe I'm too set in my ways, now that I'm retired. It doesn't matter what I think. The rest of the country seems to be hopping on the bamboo bandwagon.

Suddenly I have a vision: Procter and Gamble switches their sourcing for Charmin to bamboo. Those commercials we see with the blue cartoon bears cleaning their bums? Gone. The new ones feature pandas. Chewing on bamboo shoots on one end, wiping their tushies with bamboo TP on the other. Is this a great country, or what?

Retirees' Superstitions

Original Post Date Nov. 2, 2013

Halloween weekend is a good time to take a look at retirees' superstitions. At first blush, they seem the same as everyone else's odd beliefs, but there are differences. Moreover, the counter measures a retiree must take to neutralize bad karma aren't always what you'd expect.

True, *walking under a ladder* brings anyone negative juju. But for us, that means our Social Security check will be auto-deposited into someone else's account. We can prevent this by turning in a clockwise circle six times, but don't do this while you're under the ladder. And be sure there's a post to grab onto or a seat nearby, since you'll be dizzy after all that spinning.

Here's another well-known superstition: *break a mirror* and you'll have seven years of bad luck. For us, it starts with the doctor who has been our GP for 30 years deciding to retire. We can disrupt the spell by immediately shouting his (or her) name out loud seven times. Muttering or murmuring it doesn't work, by the way.

You might think that if you *step on a crack* in the sidewalk, you'll "break someone's back," but you would be mistaken. If you're a retiree, your bunion will have a painful flare-up, unless you go home and clip your toenails right away. The fact that you can't reach your toes won't exempt you from doing this. Best to have a toenail-clipping partner lined up. You might try the same person who plucks the goat hairs from your chin.

Spilling salt brings specific distress to retirees, unless they throw some of it over their right shoulder. If not, the next time the bridge club meets at their place, their dog will fart under the card table. The kind of rips my brother used to call "silent, but deadly." Fat chance you can convince the ladies it was really Bowser's doing.

Everyone is familiar with the notion that a *black cat crossing one's path* brings bad luck. Those of a certain age, on the other hand, know that if a black car parks in front of our house, we'll be going to a funeral soon. What most of us *don't* know is that if we immediately adopt a black cat, the funeral procession will pass us by. At least for awhile.

When you're ready to go for a walk, be sure to put your sport shoe on the *right foot first*. Otherwise, your health insurance will be canceled. Don't worry: you can counter the left-foot screw-up by following the good luck superstition of wearing your underwear inside out for a week. (You can change the underwear; just be sure to put the new pair on inside out, too.) I do this accidentally now and then, which could explain why I usually have no trouble finding a parking spot.

When your *palm itches*, do you think you're going to come into some money? Not exactly. We seniors are about to win a "free" two-day cruise to Bermuda. Take it, and your house will be burglarized while you're away. *Nose itchy?* Don't worry about getting into a physical fight, but your condo board is going to revoke your community gardening privileges. Do the *bottom of your feet itch*? Don't expect to make a trip. This one is not a superstition. Go out and buy some Gold Bond powder.

Be very careful about *opening up an umbrella indoors*. The only known retiree's antidote for that mistake is rotating a coffee cup clockwise three times, and then immediately counter-clockwise one time. The cup has to be filled with freshly brewed coffee; those Keurig pods won't work. You must follow this action by knocking on wood twice. It has to be solid wood, not those laminated, engineered products, or the ersatz composite stuff. I almost forgot: you need to do all of this in 30 seconds.

I'll continue to research superstitions, debunking the myths, finding those that apply specifically to retirees, and uncovering steps we can take to undo the voodoo. In the meantime, you all be careful out there. It's a scary world.

Movie Rating System
for Retirees

Original Post Date Dec. 14, 2013

One of the most popular forms of entertainment for retirees is going to the movies, especially on Senior Discount Day. The two key seasons for movie releases are the summer months and December. If you're planning to see a film during those periods, you should familiarize yourself with the new rating system for retirees.

If the movie you'll be seeing is rated B, make sure you go to the Bathroom just before you take your seat. You should also refrain from drinking any liquids for at least three hours prior to show time. A B rating indicates either an extremely long feature (2 1/2 hours plus) or lots of scenes with beverages being consumed. Enough said.

A rating of H alerts you to be sure your Hearing aid has fresh batteries and the volume is set to the maximum. Films given an H either are filled with soft-spoken dialogue or have a cacophony of sounds that overlap. Either way, it's hard to keep up if you miss even one line. Be sure to adjust your aid to the setting that filters out background noise.

To better enjoy a feature that carries a D rating, wear your Distance glasses. It was shot in what the cinematographer calls the "artistic style." Beauty is in the eye of the beholder, and one person's "artistic" is another person's eyestrain. Most scenes will be either darkly lit or out of focus, much like highways appear at night at our age. My distance glasses have become my cinematic essential, especially for a D flic. My viewing challenge is remembering to bring them into the theater from the car.

If you're catching a movie rated I and you're not up on pop culture, bring a younger friend to act as an Interpreter. Otherwise, you'll have trouble keeping up with the lingo and the visual jokes. If you're as pop savvy as I am, but the person you usually bring along with you (read: husband) is out of touch (read: totally clueless), you might want to attend an I film alone. Or else sit in the back of the theater so you won't disturb others as you patiently explain (and re-explain) what's going on.

The S rating stands for "Snoozefest," which you'll be at risk of having if you don't drink at least 16 ounces of a caffeinated beverage during the previews. You're probably wondering why you'd even go to see a feature that's an S. Sometimes we're not masters of our own destiny. Drink up! Just be sure to hit the bathroom when you're done gulping.

Warning: R does not stand for Retiree-friendly. It means Restricted, aka Raunchy, and no one under 17 can attend without a parent. R is not as bad as NC-17, which is almost porn and cannot be attended by anyone 17 or under, period. The retiree equivalent is the NC-80 flic, which cannot be attended by anyone 80 or older. NC-80 was set up to prevent the elderly from having a coronary in the middle of especially graphic sex scenes. Apparently the rating board never heard what goes on in The Villages in Florida.

The commonly-seen PG indicates that a movie is relatively innocent. Retirees have the GP rating, which stands for GrandParent. GP features are ideal for an outing with your grandchildren. You won't long for a 5-second delay on the dialogue. You won't need to keep one hand at the ready to cover young eyes. Best of all, the story line will be entertaining enough to keep you awake (and bathroom free) for about an hour and a half. (Films longer than that have a GP-X rating, for "extended.")

Speaking of X, our final rating for retirees is the new X. The old X was replaced by the NC-17, a trademark controlled by the Motion Picture Association of America. The new X is loosely controlled by AARP. The X still stands for "eXplicit," but what's shown is not graphic sexual content. It's close-ups of bunions, wrinkles and sagging body parts. If you see enough of this in your real life and don't care to see more of it in the theater, avoid an X-rated flic like you do caffeine after 3 pm.

There you have it, a comprehensive guide to movie ratings for retirees. Refer to it when selecting your seasonal entertainment. Be sure to collect the appropriate movie-viewing tools. Or, you could just stay home and turn on the TV. The snacks are less expensive, and the line to the bathroom is shorter.

Cinnabon Craze

Original Post Date Mar. 29, 2014

Awhile ago I wrote a post on the kale frenzy. Now I'm reporting on the Cinnabon craze. You know, that sweet confection that lures you into the shop on the concourse when you're headed to your plane. I can't resist Cinnabons, even though they pack on more calories than I burn off en route to my flight. This despite the fact that my gate is always at the far end of the walkway.

I can't explain the allure of the Cinnabon. Maybe it's the swirly intermingling of cinnamon and icing, or that soft, yeasty mouthful you get. Since I haven't been flying much now that I'm retired, I had almost forgotten about my guilty pleasure. That was, until I read in *Ad Age* about products entering into licensing arrangements with the makers of this jewel. Apparently, lip balm and the Cinnapretzel movie-theater snack didn't do well, but Air Wick and Pinnacle vodka still have projects in the oven.

The *Ad Age* article got me thinking about what products for retirees would be improved via a marriage with Cinnabon. My problem was not coming up with ideas. It was weeding out the weaker ones and focusing on the sure winners. I wouldn't want mine to land on the reject heap with the lip balm and Cinnapretzel.

The first product I'll produce is Cinnabon Odor Eaters. One of the worst offenses of older folks is smelly feet. Imagine if they gave off that delightful Cinnabon aroma instead! And the farther you walk, the stronger the smell. This will be especially useful to those traveling by air and having gate assignments like B19 and C22. It will also provide motivation to get more exercise.

Speaking of which, a companion product will be the Cinnabon treadmill roller. There's a psychological aspect to this, too, because it will remind you of what hooked you on Cinnabons to begin with. It simulates running down the concourse to catch your flight. The longer you stay on the machine, the more realistic it is. Program in a hypothetical but realistic gate number—26 say—and the mat will keep on rolling (and emitting that wonderful scent) until you've run as much as you would have in the airport.

An incentive to keep those pounds off is the Cinnabon digital scale. In addition to announcing your weight when you step on this electronic device, it will give off a burst of that mouth-watering smell. If you program it properly, the more you've lost, the stronger the explosion. As you get closer to your target weight, you'll get a staccato of bursts. This will be a true test of your willpower.

The new product that will be most of interest to retirees is my Cinnabon Velcro. Each time you unhook the pieces, you'll get a whiff of Cinnabon. My neighbors will find me sitting on my porch steps, pulling and reattaching, tongue hanging out of my mouth. They'll know I'm there before they see (or smell) me. The telltale "rip-smoosh-rip-smoosh" will give me away.

Two items that will motivate me to clean more often are Cinnabon Windex and Cinnabon Pledge. Instead of the boring orange or lemon that those products usually have, mine will smell of cinnamon, iced sugar and freshly baked yeast bread. I'll have the cleanest windows in the neighborhood. My sinuses will benefit as well, since there won't be as much dust around the house.

Here's one for all you cat owners: Cinnabon litter. When Luke (my boy) scratches, the pellets will release that delightful fragrance. The formula will be strong enough to mask that other "delightful fragrance" that announces he's had his daily constitutional. This will be a much pleasanter alert that his bathroom station needs scooping.

A personal favorite is the Cinnabon mouse pad. The more I roll my mouse over it, the stronger the aroma. I'll be writing up a storm, but my posts will likely have much more food-related content. It's a good thing my office is nowhere near the pantry.

Finally, I'm working with the Post Office to develop a Cinnabon postage stamp. We'll make it the type you have to lick, so you'll feed two senses and get a double fix. Unfortunately, these stamps will have a "use by" date, so they won't last forever. Let's face it: at our age, not much lasts forever anyway.

Red Velvet Fever

Original Post Date May 24, 2014

A few months back I was salivating over the Cinnabon craze. I shared a number of product line extensions and licenses introduced by the owner of that trademark. I also had some sweet ideas of my own. Today's post is in a similar vein. It was inspired by the *NY Times* article: "Red Velvet Cake: A Classic, not a Gimmick." In my shrine of confectionary treasures, Red Velvet Cake (RVC) would be right up there next to the Cinnabon.

The *Times* article describes RVC as having "cocoa undertones and cream-cheese tang" that can easily be recreated in a lab. Adams Extract Company markets an RV cake mix complete with bottles of the extract and red dye. Some of the non-edible RVC products available are the predictable scented candles and air fresheners. Less yawn-inducing are the body mist and red velvet vodka.

As I did with the Cinnabon, I've conjured up some products for retirees that incorporate the undertones and tang of red velvet. I doubt any of my ideas will outshine the red velvet waffles served at Freddy J's BBQ in Buffalo, but here goes.

The first items on my list are **Red Velvet Bath Sponges and Shower Poufs**. Retirees are sometimes tempted to substitute a quick sink-side swish of the important areas for a full shower on days when we have no plans to go out. Our dermatologists may even have suggested that our aging skin will fare better without a ritual scrubbing every day. It will be hard to resist a hot shower, or even a lukewarm bath, if the aroma of RVC is wafting in the air. Your unexpected guests will thank me for this.

Taking the body mist idea into a more functional mode, **RVC Insect Repellent** will allow us to lounge a bit longer on the patio at sundown without fear of being "eaten alive," as my mother used to say. The RVC formulation will be so treacly that most mosquitos will want no part of it. Those that are brave enough to land on your skin will keel over from cloying nostrils, or whatever part of the anatomy an insect breathes through.

Seniors will be especially excited to try **Powdered RVC Psyllium Husks**. This new source of fiber is expected to sell three times the volume of orange-flavored Metamucil. I can't believe Procter & Gamble has owned that staple of retirement for almost thirty years and they never thought of a RVC line extension.

I'm also hopping on one of the hottest beverage crazes, energy drinks, by introducing RVC Vitamin Water. Actually, I can't call it Vitamin Water; that's a trademark. So I'll call it **Red Velvet Cake Vigor Eau**. Rhymes with Figaro. Google tells me there's a men's cologne called Vigor, or more correctly: Vigor Eau de Toilette. But since you don't drink that (or at least, you're not supposed to), I think I'll be OK with my RVC Vigor Eau.

If the reason you crave Vigor Eau is that you've been exercising strenuously, there's a good chance (as an older person) that you've sprained something and need to wear an Ace bandage for awhile. To help take the sting out of the experience, I've created a **Red Velvet Cake Elastic Wrap**. Every time you unroll it and stretch it around your sprain, you get a fresh whiff of RVC. Almost makes it worth working out. I said almost.

One of my favorite new products are my **Red Velvet Slipper Socks**, and not just because they are, of course, red. They're knitted of chenille yarn soaked in genuine red velvet extract from the Adams Extract Company. The toes have packets of cream-cheese-flavored body lotion so they moisturize while you walk. If your partner has a foot fetish, expect lots of massages and some toe-licking—a win-win. Or not.

Finally, I'm line extending one of the items I developed in response to the Cinnabon Craze. Soon you'll be able to buy **Red Velvet Cake Postage Stamps**. As with the Cinnabon ones, they'll be the type you have to lick. So they'll not only smell good, they'll taste great. I've decided these stamps are such a brilliant idea that I'm working on an Americana Baked Goods collection for the USPS. In addition to the Cinnabon and RVC, you'll get Carrot Cake and Strawberry Shortcake stamps—four options on one block! You can thank me later.

Revisionist Recreation
for Retirees

Original Post Date Jun. 6, 2014

If you're looking for low-stress recreation, now is a great time to be retiring. Changes that are afoot for golf and chess will make both of these activities more senior-friendly.

Courses around the country are testing revisions aimed at making golf more relaxing for seniors. "Aimed" is the operative word here. Those who are especially unskilled at putting that little white ball into that almost-as-little cup are a key audience for this trend.

The lead to an April *N. Y. Times* article by Bill Pennington got my attention: "Golf holes the size of pizzas." Pennington tells us that industry leaders worry about golf "following the baby boomer generation into the grave." This is not an image I want in my head as I watch golf on Sunday afternoon TV. To re-quote pro Sergio Garcia on the new rules: "A 15-inch hole could help… older golfers score better." Ya think? And don't expect me to dig deeper into scoring in a 15-inch hole. You can go there on your own.

Another idea being kicked around is foot golf, using soccer balls, along with those pizza-sized holes. A key objective is to reduce the intimidation many folks feel when confronted with golf's single set of rules for experts and amateurs alike. What's the big deal if they have a second set of rules that are more retiree-friendly? It's not like someone who wants to play just nine holes with cups that he can actually see without his driving glasses on is going to compete in a PGA sanctioned event.

The TV commentators spend a lot of time discussing a pro's club selection. I gather they can carry only a limited number of clubs in their bag during a tournament under the current rules. That sounds like an advantage to me. I'd be as confused over which club to use as I would be over which golf shoes to wear with what outfit. Give me just two clubs, but put a different head thingy on each end. If it doesn't work one way, I'll turn it upside down and try again.

Speaking of trying again, another idea being floated is to help inept players get out of especially rough spots without levying penalty shots. Mulligans for all! And for every hole. (I used to think a mulligan was a style of golf shoe, by the way.) Just kick it out of that sand hazard. Or better yet, toss it out with your ungloved hand.

Even the PGA is on board with simplifying the game, tradition be damned. But don't worry, plaid pants and wildly colored shirts will still be *de rigueur* for tournaments. Well, that's a relief.

If your participation leans more in the armchair direction, you might be interested in efforts underway to make chess a spectator sport. This tidbit was reported in the *Financial Times* global section. Andrew Paulson, an entrepreneur with very deep pockets—and loads of patience, apparently—has set off on a crusade to make this happen.

Reporter James Crabtree claims Paulson "plans to infuse chess with… sponsorship deals and… razzmatazz." As I read this, the strains of the song "Razzle Dazzle" from *Chicago* began playing in my head. *"Give 'em the old Razzle Dazzle, razzle-dazzle 'em. Long as you keep 'em way off balance, how can they spot you've got no talents? Razzle-dazzle 'em, and they'll make you a star!"*

One piece of so-called razzmatazz would be biometric bracelets worn by the players. They'd track things like heart rate and perspiration level, "giving spectators an instant sense of the stresses faced at the board." I don't know about you, but I'm all tingly with anticipation just thinking about this.

Paulson is quoted as saying: *"If you can persuade millions to watch golf, chess is going to be an easy sell."* Not so fast, Paulson. If you'd read Pennington's article, you'd know that golf isn't such an easy sell anymore, either. Maybe if they add mulligans to chess, we'd get some real excitement. *"Oops! You just captured my queen. My bad. I'd like a do-over, thank you."*

Crabtree put his finger on the biggest stumbling block to making chess must-see TV. Sponsors are giving it a wide berth because the man who has run the sport for decades is an eccentric, to put it mildly. Perhaps this is due to the fact that (according to him) aliens once abducted him. On the plus side, they sent him back to earth with the knowledge that they had created the game of chess. You just can't make this stuff up. Well, maybe you can. But this time I didn't. Honest.

10 Reasons Newspapers Are Better Than E-Papers

Original Post Date Sep. 13, 2014

Conventional newspapers are struggling to stay in business. To paraphrase the Ikea ad for its "book book" catalog, readers of "paper papers" are increasingly migrating to e-papers, the electronic versions of the daily press. E-papers may be convenient, but there are certain things that they can never do that the printed versions of newspapers can. Herewith 10 reasons paper papers are better than e-papers.

10. You can't utilize e-papers to pack kitchen crockery and glasses when you move.
I've used and reused more sheets than I can count this summer as we moved from our house to a temporary apartment and then to our condo.

9. You can't clean windows with e-papers and a spray bottle of ammonia water.
A *Household Hints for the Budget Conscious* list that's worth it's salt will always include this as a cost effective way to clean glass around the house.

8. You can't cut an e-paper into the same sizes as your framed prints and tape them to the wall behind your couch so you can plan the layout without making holes.
This tried and true method for perfect picture

placement is yet another way that paper papers come in handy when you're relocating.

7. You can't use a rolled-up e-paper to discipline a puppy during potty training (and you can't spread it out where the puppy tends to make its mistakes).

Remember: just a gentle tap on the puppy's snout. Not his fanny and never a hard hit.

6. You can't swat horseflies with a rolled-up e-paper.

Yes, it's tough to swat flies with a rolled up newspaper, but if you're persistent, you can at least scare them to someone else's table.

5. You can't wad up an e-paper and stuff it into the toes of your wet hiking boots to dry them out.

Ditto for your street shoes that got soaked when you tried to jump the puddles in the road and missed.

4. You can't insulate your long underwear with an e-paper when you're camping.

And if you're a senior, you probably wear long underwear all winter, camping or not.

3. You won't find an e-paper cut into squares and nailed to the wall of a water closet in a one-star *pensione* in Europe.

In the late '60's, I traveled with my own roll of TP. It was especially useful with the toilets that were just a hole in the ground. Two-star *pensiones* had porcelain floor plates with footprints molded in, to help you straddle the hole for better aim.

2. You can't fold an e-paper into a discrete book cover for your copy of *50 Shades of Grey* when you're reading poolside at your club.
For those living under a rock, the movie version is set to release on Valentine's Day, 2015. Be sure to get your refresher read in before then. Or not.

And the number one reason a paper newspaper is better than an e-paper:

1. You can't line a litter box with an e-paper.
I pick up the free monthly papers expressly for this purpose. First a wee-wee pad. Then five or six broadsheets. Then four 1-quart saucepans of litter. And no, I don't cook with the same pan. It's just for Luke's needs.

So you see, we'd all be lost without conventional newspapers, but me especially. Please do your civic duty and buy at least one paper paper every week. You'll have my gratitude. And also Luke's.

Retirement Sparks Redux

Section IV

Retirement Tools & Tips

Curse Like A Retiree

Original Post Date Apr. 27, 2013

Some months back, *Time* magazine had one of those feature boxes that are quick and entertaining reads. It shared some choice curse phrases from Jason Sacher's book *How to Swear Around the World*. You'd have to be a holy roller not to laugh at them. My three favorites translated thusly: *"You are stupid as a broom"* (contributed by the French), *"A fart to your beard"* (a Persian specialty), and perhaps the strangest one— from Finland—*"May you piss into a transformer."*

You just know where this post is heading. IMHO, if you're going to curse at someone, you might as well be colorful and creative about it. I'm providing an array of new phrases to help you insult fellow retirees. They can also be used to offend people who are not yet retired, but probably should be.

When I was in high school, this insult was going around: *"Your mother wears combat boots."* Those in on the game would reply: *"She does not. She wears Army surplus sneakers."* This inspired my first retiree curse. *"Your walking shoes use counterfeit Velcro."* The savvy wearer will reply: *"They do not. I'm beta testing a new and improved version."*

The second phrase is a variation on a foreign localism my brother picked up in the late sixties. After his Army discharge, he crossed Northern Africa in a Volkswagon camper. When he came home, he challenged opinions not to his liking by shouting: *"May a thousand camels beat a path across your front yard."* This was followed by drumming his hands loudly on the top of the table. In that spirit, I give you: *"May a caravan of out-of-control Jazzy scooters tear a path through your vegetable garden."* Vroom! Vroom!

The Persians inspired this next one. *"May the fart you laid turn out not to be a fart after all on the very day you ran out of Depends."* Think about that one... Or maybe don't.

Here's one that heaps insult upon injury. *"Your grandchildren are so dumb, they don't even know how ugly they are."* You may want to step back a few yards as you hurl that one.

"The Smithsonian requisitioned your earwax for their collections" is a good start. For maximum effect, follow up with *"They're displaying it next to the amber from Jurassic Park."*

Here are three especially tailored to retirees. *"May your pension fund manager make Bernie Madoff look like a Boy Scout."* *"May your Social Security payments get auto-deposited into someone else's account."* *"May your shredder short-circuit and destroy all your Medicare paperwork."*

Then there's the Irish prayer turned insult: *"May the road rise up to meet your face when you trip on your daily walk."* Or perhaps more accurately, may your face fall down to meet the road...

Of course, there are the more obvious insults that focus on physical characteristics. There's *Old Gnarly Toes* and *Gizzard Neck*, and for someone who is peppered with liver spots, *Domino Face*. But they're not really creative; they're just mean. Try something more unusual, like: *"Didn't anyone tell you you're supposed to eat prunes, not wear them?"* Or one that's more with the times, like: *"Your face could crash the Skype network."*

It's always good to tailor the curse to something specific about the person you're aiming it at. *"May you get arrested for flashing a plumber's butt when the elastic in your Sansabelts gives way."*

Perhaps the worst curse I can imagine directed at me is: *"May your chin bristles spread to your nostrils and your ears."* Not a pretty picture. But it's way better than: *"May a thousand camels piss into your cat's litter box."*

Retirees' Uses for Duct Tape and WD-40

Original Post Date Aug. 03, 2013

We're all familiar with that old saw: use duct tape for things that are supposed to stick together, but won't; use WD-40 for things that aren't supposed to stick together, but do. This is one of the great truisms of life. As my retirement time accumulates, so do my uses for these awesome products.

You may have noticed that I complain about the goat hairs on my chin. Now I also have duck fuzz that's looking increasingly like sideburns. None of this is hair that I celebrate. I'm uneasy about those waxing strips you see on late-night TV. Older skin is more sensitive to temperature extremes. Plus that wax stuff would eat into my wine budget. I decided to try duct tape to remove my unwanted hair. It was cost effective and it lived up to its reputation.

Here are some tips I developed after doing this several times. Fold over the end of the duct tape about 1/2 inch before you stick it to your face. It makes it easier to grab when you pull it off. If it's humid when you do your toilette, first open the door of your freezer and stick your head in for a few minutes. It will cool you down so you don't perspire. Ice cubes won't work, because they leave your skin damp, preventing the tape from adhering.

Do you slip more often on your non-carpeted stairs now that you're of a certain age? Cut strips of duct tape about 6 inches long and form loops, sticky side out. Place these on your steps where the ball of your foot usually lands. You may need to make a test run, to find the best placement. Now when you go up and down, the duct tape will grip your foot or shoes (or especially socks!) just enough to slow you down so you can keep your balance. Replenish tape as it gets fuzzy.

WD-40 can also make your life easier. Do you have difficulty getting your street shoes on? Stop exerting yourself! Don't risk a heart attack. Spray the inside of the shoe, especially the heel area, with WD-40. Also spray your feet, whether you're wearing socks or not. You'll glide in like butter. For maximum benefit, do one shoe and one foot at a time. Make a note: if you have heart issues, the cost of the WD-40 may qualify for a medical deduction.

Ladies, in swim season, WD-40 will be your new best friend when it comes to the on-and-off process of swimwear. (Think pool and beach restrooms...) Spray your outer thighs, hips, butt cheeks and belly with a liberal amount. Your suit will slip on and off like silk. This also works for Spanx at any time of year. WD-40 comes in a purse-size container that I'm sure was made just for this purpose.

Here's a slightly more complicated use for duct tape. If you're at all sensitive about your private parts, skip the next two paragraphs. If you're not terribly good with engineering, you might want to refer to the schematic provided.

Older men often have difficulty keeping the boys tucked in where they belong. Duct tape to the rescue! Cut a piece about ten inches long and another about four inches. Place the four-inch piece in the center of the ten-inch one, tacky sides together. This provides a sling for the guys that won't stick to them. Carefully cradle them in the center of the tape and lift them to where you want them. Press the sticky side of the three-inch long end pieces against your groin area. You might want to shave first.

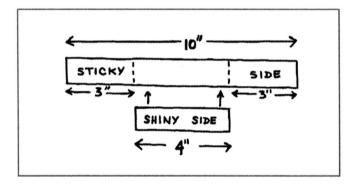

Older women have a similar problem keeping their girls perky. Make two slings similar to the one described above for men. If your cup runneth over, you may need longer pieces of tape (and a longer sling area). Just be sure to allow three sticky inches on each end.

Here are more uses for WD-40 that you've probably never considered. Having trouble lately turning the pages of books you're reading because the paper sticks together? Do bill stubs refuse to go into the envelopes provided to mail the payment? Spray them with WD-40, but don't overspray. Let them dry a bit, then turn the pages of the book with ease, or slide the stub into the envelope without having to tear it apart.

Have you noticed that adding fabric softener to the wash is just one more thing you're forgetting these days? Too much static on things coming out of the dryer? Spray the legs of your polyester pants (or other non-silk garments) with WD-40 and your sausage-cling problems are over.

Duct tape and WD-40: Miracle tools for people of all ages. Just think outside the box. Or can. And off the roll.

Special Senior Allowances

Original Post Date Oct. 5, 2013

A few days back, my husband was sitting next to me at the breakfast table when I noticed that he had a sticker affixed to his eyeglasses. I wondered what that was about. Turns out it was the magnification number. I asked if he kept it on the glasses as a sort of announcement, and did he think he would get some type of special treatment because he wears 3.0 magnifiers.

Of course he didn't, but that gave me an idea. We should get price reductions on things because of our diminishing eyesight. Call it a "Visual Acuity Discount" for seniors. This led me to develop a list of various allowances to which seniors should be entitled.

I was 66 and change before I learned that a local market gives 5% senior discounts on Tuesdays. "Not too bad," thought I. "I've only missed out on about a year of savings." Turns out I missed out on 11 years because of my ignorance. They begin this privilege when you turn 55. I want our allowances to go beyond that standard day-of-the-week percent off. I want special treatment for senior circumstances every day.

We'll start with that "**Visual Acuity Discount**." Anyone who wears glasses with a magnification level of 3.0 or higher will get eBooks for free from Kindle. They'll also get to make younger people give up their seats in the primo rows at the movie theater when they arrive so late that only the first three rows or the last six have seats together. That's not a discount, but it's even better than one.

There's also the "**Gray Hair Respect Grant.**" You're entitled to some respect when your hair is anywhere from totally gray to having 3/4" of gray roots showing. (That would be me most of the time.) Under this grant, you go straight to the front of the line at the bank, the post office, the DMV, or at any other facility run by the government or by a quasi-governmental entity. There isn't any special consideration for bald men. Too many young bucks shave their heads today.

The "**Meandering Balance**" decreases in proportion to a senior's feebleness. The amount you pay is calculated by dividing the forward progress by the horizontal movement getting there. If you teeter-totter sideways across a two-feet wide space in order to move 8 inches forward, your ratio is 8 divided by 24, or one third. A ten-dollar item will cost you just $3.33. The more decrepit you become, the wider you'll teeter, reducing your Meandering Balance and lowering your prices.

Older folks acquire more bruises, especially post-retirement, when they spend more time in that most-dangerous of all places: home. Fortunately, there's an upside to this. Flash just one black-and-blue mark to get the "**Bruise Allowance**" at any health club, fitness center or sports facility.

One of the easiest senior considerations to snag is the "**Medication Provision**." Provide proof that you're on just one prescription for a chronic condition and you automatically go to the head of the line at emergency rooms, movie theaters and the dressing rooms at all national discount clothing chains. Lipitor, Plavix, Lisinopril, Fosamax—all qualify you. Sorry, but Viagra and Cialis are regarded as treatments for acute shortcomings; if that's all you've got, you'll just have to wait your turn.

The "**Vertigo Variance**" is provided to seniors who get dizzy if they stand up from a prone position without a midway rest stop. It allows them to show up as much as an hour late for meetings, doctors' appointments, lunch dates—anything with a fixed time when they're supposed to be there. Documented stages of vertigo are coded to match Affordable Care Health Insurance. That is: bronze (15 minutes late), silver (1/2 hour), gold (45 minutes) and platinum (one hour late).

The "**Age Spot Accommodation**" is determined by the number and density of the liver spot patterns on visible skin (generally, your hands and face). Total the number of clearly visible spots you have. Multiply that by the number of distinct areas of spot patterns. The result is your accommodation score. For every one hundred points, you get 10% off your purchase at any participating retailer. Do the math: If your points exceed 1,000, you get stuff for free. I am so there.

These special allowances for seniors will significantly improve our lives. You have to wonder why no one thought of them before. This post pretty much wrote itself. All it took was some careful observation of the seniors around me (and in my mirror). Well, that and a few glasses of wine.

Shapewear for Retirees

Original Post Date Nov. 23, 2013

Good news for retirees who are struggling to get their BMI (Body Mass Index) under control. There's new shapewear that's supposed to help us burn off fat.

We now have at our disposal exercise pants and other items that are infused with caffeine to help us lose weight. When I learned about these, my first thought was: *I've heard of transdermal delivery of medications, but this is ridiculous.* My second thought was: *If it works, why don't we just soak in a tubful of coffee?*

I researched this before I decided to report on it. I uncovered several companies that are marketing caffeine-infused shapewear. There's Lytess, French makers of leggings, and SkinKiss Limited in the UK, offering caffeine tights and shapewear.

The UK's *Daily Mail* reported on another French company that makes the line Top Model from designer Simone Pérèle. I assumed Simone was a "top model" in France, but it turns out she was a corsetière. She obtained her diploma in corset making in 1935; after the war, she specialized in made-to-order lingerie, especially bras. Her children now run the company.

I digress. The supposed science behind these caffeine-infused garments was reported in 2006 research at Vanderbilt University. Authors Minnette Boesel and Professor Schlundt claim that caffeine "helps blood flow to the skin and works like a diuretic, flushing moisture out of the skin and firming it." Actually, the quote comes from the editor of *Allure Magazine*, which makes one suspicious of the scientific cred of this study.

Topicals that make these claims usually contain not just caffeine, but also vitamin E, retinol, aloe vera and even fennel and *gotu kola* (whatever that is). I'll tell you what that is. It's a swamp plant found in India, Sri Lanka and Indonesia. Its leaves and stems are used in traditional Chinese and Ayurvedic medicine. Several websites emphasize that *gotu kola* is not the same as the kola nut; *gotu kola* does not have caffeine and is not a stimulant. On that edifying note, let's return to the Vanderbilt study.

Boesel concluded that while "some of these lotions and potions with caffeine may have some effect on the *appearance* of cellulite as a result of dehydration... the results are temporary and do nothing to banish the presence of cellulite." So what. The results may not last forever, but let's face it: nothing does anymore. Back now to the caffeine-infused shapewear.

According to *Good Morning America*, the makers claim that Lytess leggings can take as much as "two inches off your hips and more than an inch from your thighs just by wearing them for 5 hours a day for 21 days." Plus, they don't smell like coffee, and they don't keep you up at night. I don't know about you, but I'd sit up bug-eyed for three weeks if it would take two inches off my hips. The company claims it "has sold 3.5 million pairs of the pants in France to satisfied customers." I'll bet they're satisfied!

SkinKiss.com says that its products "contain Microcapsules of Caffeine that have slimming benefits" and that their "caffeine tights have won critical acclaim." There was no elaboration on the specifics of the benefits or the source of the acclaim. The *Daily Mail* tells us that Top Model caffeine-infused microfiber shapewear "blasts cellulite." An independent 28-day study reports "63% of women tested it and said it was effective." Oh, and the effects last for 100 washes, at $50 to $80 a pop.

If your lingerie budget is as skimpy as mine post-retirement, you'll probably want to look into other ways to control your BMI before you jump into the caffeine panties. To that end, see my post on yoga exercises for seniors (Section I).

In the meantime, I'm going to see if anyone is developing nicotine-infused shapewear as a way to help folks quit smoking. I'm not a smoker, but I bet there's a fortune to be made in replacing cigarettes with nico panties. If I can get in on the ground floor of this with even a modest investment, I'll probably be able to afford caffeine panties. And more expensive wine. What can I say? I'm just an entrepreneur at heart.

Budgeting Tools
Original Post Date Mar. 1, 2014

One of the most important skills a recent or soon-to-be retiree must master is budgeting. First you have to determine how much income you can reasonably count on after you stop working full time. Then you have to figure out how you'll spend it. Alternately, you can decide what you need (or want) to spend in retirement, and then wrack your brain over where the heck that amount of money will come from. Which generally leads to rethinking how much you really need to spend.

There are many books and websites to help with this planning. But few provide tools to help you sequester your funds into the categories you've identified in your retirement budget. A commercial from the financial services company ING (now Voya) offers an unusual suggestion. Money earmarked for retirement is colored orange (the same as ING's logo). That doesn't seem practical. Plus U.S. Code Title 18 Section 333 tells us it's illegal to deface U.S. currency.

Specifically: *"Whoever mutilates,... disfigures, or... does any other thing to any bank bill... issued by... the Federal Reserve System, with intent to render such... unfit to be reissued, shall be fined... or imprisoned not more than six months, or both."* There's room for interpretation about what rendering money "unfit to be reissued" means, but I don't think Uncle Sam would look kindly on dying our money orange.

That left me pondering other tools to help retirees set aside income earmarked for specific expenses. I'm reminded of something from my childhood. When I was 3, we moved from a suburb of Newark, New Jersey to live year round in the summer cottage my father had built in northern Jersey. He winterized it gradually and for years we had a potbellied stove in the living room to provide extra heat.

At the time, my father's method of budgeting was manila envelopes. Every payday, he put cash into "files" labeled mortgage, groceries, oil, etc. The stove was still with us in the early 1950's when he finally opened a checking account. The Federal Reserve Bank of Atlanta's website tells us: "Checking accounts in the United States almost doubled between 1939 and 1952," so my father was a late adopter. The FRBA site credits the growth after 1952 to the advent of MICR (Magnetic Ink Character Recognition).

MICR not withstanding, I'm not sure what led to the switch from cash to checks in our household. We lived in God's country, with just a Catholic Church and a bar (the neighborhood essentials) in our hamlet. My father commuted to work by car about three hours a day round trip. Perhaps a bank branch with convenient hours opened *en route*. What I do know is he ceremoniously burned the now-obsolete manila envelopes in the potbelly.

I must have been around 7 then and I was thrilled to be allowed to help out. My father retrieved any important contents from the envelopes and gave the empties to me to bundle for him to burn. Imagine my excitement when I discovered a five-dollar bill still inside one! I didn't get to keep the money, but I never forgot the "attaboy" from my father. (He did not bestow praise gratuitously.)

Looking back, I realize my mother was probably behind the switch to checking. She might have had her eye on one of those toasters that banks gave out in the early fifties for newly opened accounts. More likely she decided she wanted to free up space in the living room, because the stove disappeared soon after the burning ritual.

This brings me to some tools for sequestering money into budgeted slots. One solution (an improved version of my father's manila envelopes) is to put the cash into see-thru Ziploc bags marked for each item. You can also use empty pill bottles. Match the vitamin letter to the budget category: E for electric, C for cell phone. Or prescriptions: Hydrocodone for house repairs, Lisinopril for lawn care, Lipitor for lattes, Plavix for physicians. You get the idea.

I especially like the Sock Solution, because it takes care of another problem: mismatched socks. Ones whose mate disappeared, but as soon as you discard it, the lost one shows up. Stuff your cash into socks labeled for each budget category. Knot the ends and stow them in a drawer marked "Budget."

I could go on, but just pick your favorite method. Or open a checking account just for money earmarked for specific needs. The bank might even give you a thermal mug. Or a polar fleece blanket. But don't expect a toaster.

Hail Marys and Late Life Pouts
Original Post Date Mar. 15, 2014

The *New York Times* ran an article titled "The Hail-Mary-Moon." The phrase is a take off on the Hail-Mary-Pass. For those who need it, I give you this definition of the football play from Wikipedia. *"The Hail May pass... is a very long forward pass... made in desperation with only a small chance of success, especially at or near the end of a half."*

Wikipedia tells us the phrase originally meant *"any sort of desperation play."* The long-pass meaning became popular thanks to Roger Staubach, then quarterback of the Dallas Cowboys. After his 1975 playoff-game-winning touchdown pass, Staubach (a good Catholic boy) was quoted as saying: *"I closed my eyes and said a Hail Mary."* The pass was thrown from midfield with just 32 seconds left in the game. My thoughts on reading this: "Wow! There were playoff games in December in the seventies."

Getting back to that "any sort of desperation play" definition, we return to The Hail-Mary-Moon (also sometimes called a save-cation). The article's author, Carrie Seim, reports that for some pairs: *"egged on by couples' therapists and travel agents, the best way to address a rift in the marriage, and to see whether it can be healed, is to take a last-ditch vacation."* Having therapists and travel agents pushing these trips raises a red flag in a relationship battle for me, not a white one.

Seim provides an example of a couple married 20 years who saved their marriage by taking a cruise to Mexico. Other couples fared not so well. One pair who traveled with their best friends not only got divorced after the trip, they wound up trading partners. It seems the swaperoo was kindled during the stay-cation for two of them. The tossed aside spouses eventually found love again—with each other. Someone needs to make up a clever moon name for that outcome.

It seems a few folks try the Hail-Mary-Moon because they think it will be cheaper than a divorce. Talk about something done *"in desperation with only a small chance of success."* Call me a cynic, but if you're doing this because of your wallet, I think you need more like a Novena-Moon.

Apparently it's not just the authors of newspaper articles that noticed this trend. Screenwriters are onto it, too. A new film called *Le Week-End* follows an older British couple who decide to spend their 30th wedding anniversary where they went on their honeymoon—Paris. Their expectation is to either refurbish their frayed marriage or face the fact that the music is over. I've not seen the movie, but it sounds like they go on a roller-coaster ride of emotions and expectations.

The site *RogerEbert.com* awards the film three and a half stars (out of four), but the *LATimes.com* snarks that it is "sour and misanthropic" and "unremittingly bleak." This contrast in reviews strikes me as an apt metaphor for many marriages that are coming unraveled: one partner finds the daily familiarity to be peachy; the other picks at the sour grapes of predictability.

To up your chances of success rekindling a fading romance, check out *Elle.com's* "Real Beauty." The subject of a recent email read: "How to get the perfect crimson pout." *Elle.com* tells us: "When it comes to makeup, nothing rivals the power of a red lip. A crimson pout will... up your sex factor." I'll bet. The article lists the red lipstick choices of ten celebrities, but not much else.

I found helpful advice on *lifestyle.ca.msn.com*. From makeup artist Emily Kate Warren: "Gently rub lips with a warm, wet washcloth before you apply any color." The site tells us to "let your lips go a bit slack" to get an even application. According to CoverGirl makeup artist Molly Stern, "Puckering too much makes it hard to get a perfect finish." I don't know about you, but I've always avoided over-puckering.

The take away from all of this seems to be that, if your marriage has become too comfortable, you need to escape your daily rut to get a fresh start. Other than the clever "moon" label and new lipstick colors, I'm not sure why this is newsworthy. It stands to reason that if a relationship is no longer working, you need to change things up. Either get away separately, or go away together. And call it whatever.

Frankly, I'd be happy to claim that my marriage is on the rocks if I thought it would get me a trip to Paris. I'll go with or without my husband, though I'd prefer with. If it will help make it happen, I'll say ten *Hail Marys*. Glory be and hallelujah! Excuse me while I go practice my pout.

Benefits of Sitting
Original Post Date Mar. 22, 2014

For some reason the media are re-publicizing the health dangers of sitting for long periods of time. The list I heard on *Live with Kelly and Michael* had about ten items on it. The ones that stood out were back pains, circulatory problems (including blood clots) and constipation. In my experience, constipation and back pain usually come in tandem, so I'm not sure they should be counted as separate dangers.

In any case, this itemization of negatives completely missed the positives. As a retiree who spends more and more time sitting down, I'm compelled to put forth the contrarian argument. Staying in one place is good for your health.

Let's face it. The older we get, the harder it is to remember whether we're coming or going. I think it has something to do with blood rushing downstream when we stand up, leaving less of it to fuel our brain cells. Retirees' gray matter needs more oxygen, not less, so standing and walking become a detriment to our mental health.

If we're lucky enough to figure out where we're headed, there's a good chance we won't remember why it was we went there once we arrive. That's due in part to the "event boundary" factor, which should be familiar to those who read my post: "Thresholds, Stairs and Memory Loss" (Section VI).

A logical extension of all of this is that when we're done with whatever, we can't remember where we're supposed to go back to, either. You don't need fully-oxygenated gray matter to see where I'm headed (narratively, not physically; I'm sitting down). There are clear benefits to plopping your fanny in a comfortable chair for hours at a time.

The most obvious one is that you never have to wonder if you're coming or going, or where to or from, because you're already there. The net result is less stress, lower blood pressure and higher self esteem. All beneficial to your physical and mental health, no matter what your age.

You can enhance the benefits with a little pre-planning. Buy a convenient tote or two—the kind that handymen and gardening hobbyists carry around. Make a list of the items you use regularly: pens, scratch pads, reading glasses, lip balm, tissues, coffee mugs—you get the idea. Fasten the list securely to the side of the tote, so you won't have to hunt for it every day.

When you're ready to settle in, grab the tote and look at your list. Fill the container with everything you might want to use that day. By the way, if one of the things on the list is "book I'm reading," be sure to leave a blank line where you can pencil in the title of the book and where you set it down last. You don't want to waste valuable sitting time trying to remember what you're reading, or running around the house looking for it.

If you want to make this routine truly effective, install one of those new fangled pod machines and a supply of bottled water close to your nest. You'll have fresh coffee or tea at your fingertips.

My final hint for success: get a fat, washable marker and draw a circle around your chair to delineate the area that's within arm's length. Position your tote, your Keurig-wannabe, your book(s), craft supplies, whatever, within the circle. You'll be guaranteed to be able to reach everything without getting up off your ever-widening butt. Wider butts improve sitting stability, by the way.

The circle has an extra advantage. Anyone who is foolish enough to disturb you will know to stay beyond the marker line. Otherwise, you'll be able to smack them with the fly swatter in your tote, without having to lift an inch off your chair.

So you see, staying put can offer health advantages to your friends and family, too. For inquiring minds that want to know, I'm setting up my chair area next to my wine rack. I have an easy-to-use corkscrew and a box of very long straws in my tote.

Spices of Retirement

Original Post Date Apr. 19, 2014

Occasionally I'll read or hear an article on planning your meals so that they satisfy all five of your different taste buds. If you miss any of them, you'll walk away from the dinner table with cravings for the missing one. We're talking about sweet, sour, salty, bitter and umami (savory). If this last one is not familiar to you, think cheese or ripe tomatoes, and read up on Monosodium Glutamate (MSG).

It's not unusual for me to walk away from meals craving more. I'm not convinced it has anything to do with the five basic tastes. The diet my sister talked me into last June has me keeping a food journal, so I know exactly what I've consumed and what buds have been palpitated. After about ten months, I think I know what drives me and many other seniors to forage in the pantry and the refrigerator late at night. And in the middle of the afternoon. And sometimes even mid-morning.

When you reach retirement, you have an entirely different set of tastes to be satisfied from your culinary cupboard. It's important to address them all, or you'll spend your golden years feeling deprived, depressed, anxious and confused. You may spend those years that way anyway, but understanding the *Spices of Retirement* will make this less likely.

Family Flavor. This is the most important spice in the retirement rack. It doesn't matter if you come from a small family or a large one; or if any members live near you vs. all being far away. A meal that includes Family Flavor fills the need to feel part of a clan, to be connected to loved ones on your family tree. And even to those with whom you've had a long-standing feud. Once we reach retirement, savoring the feuds can be as fulfilling as feeling the love.

Holiday Memories. Sprinkle this one on anything on your plate, and you are instantly transported back to the most wonderful times from your youth. Holiday Memories have the flavor of every meal that was prepared with extra love. It's rich in tradition. It's also high in calories, but who cares?

Pinch of Frugality. Even retirees on a fixed budget will splurge on a fabulous meal now and then. To help you forget about how much the meal costs, be sure to have a Pinch of Frugality on your entree. As an added benefit, Frugality has a negative impact on calories. If your dessert is a calorific treat, a Pinch of Frugality on that will make it taste even sweeter.

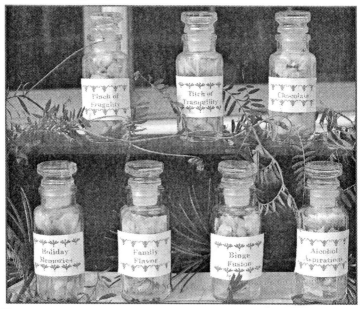

Binge Fusion. Yes, we're older, and we're told to watch what and how much we eat. Our GPs discourage us from binging. But that doesn't mean we can't have the gustatory equivalent of a binge realized via our meals or snacks. A handful of Binge Fusion will taste like any number of items that you can't eat just one of. It comes in several varieties. Pick your guilty pleasure, or lard up the pantry with several different packets of this retirement spice.

Alcohol Aspirations. Once we reach a certain age, we're also told to cut back on alcohol. Don't they realize that the older we are, the more a glass of fine wine transports us to places that can make us smile, lower our blood pressure and blot out the stressful world around us? No problem. A few drops of Alcohol Aspirations in your filtered water can give you the same result. It's not as satisfying as an actual glass of wine (what is?), but it has its advantages. (As if!)

Titch of Tranquility. No retiree's meal is complete without a Titch of Tranquility. It helps us leave the table feeling peaceful, refreshed and ready for a good nap. A small dose of Tranquility will also lower your blood pressure almost as much as a spritz of Alcohol Aspirations.

Chocolate. Period. Enough said.

There you have it. The seven essential Spices of Retirement. A meal that includes all of them is guaranteed to be as satisfying as one that tickles the five traditional taste buds. When the media finally picks up on this, remember: you read it here first.

Halloween Costumes
for Retirees

Original Post Date Oct. 25, 2014

BlogHer.com recently featured a post on Halloween costumes based on pop culture. The same day their home page quoted blogger PJ Gach: *"Jumpsuits were made by the devil with the sole purpose of not letting women pee."* The confluence of these ideas made me realize that retirees need guidelines for choosing Halloween attire. Here they are, along with some accessories ideas, just in time for you to adjust the getup you've planned for this year's trick-or-treating.

The first guideline is that, unlike jumpsuits, your costume must let you pee. One way an outfit can accommodate this is to enable you to get in and out of it easily. Look for lots of Velcro, like a straight jacket. Or something loose and flowy on the bottom, like a fortune teller's caftan. Another way is to have some highly absorbent material built in, like SpongeBob SquarePants with pants made of actual sponges.

Another important guideline is to wear comfortable, flat footwear. Running shoes or slippers are best, so choose attire that makes sense with those. You can just wear a polyester jogging suit or your ratty old bathrobe. Easy peasy.

A simple and cheap costume for a retiree is an alarm clock. It's a great way to remind your friends who are still working that you get to sleep in. Mark the clock face "alarm" and set the time to 10 am. On your back, wear an empty cardboard box marked "battery compartment." Leave it open, showing just the space with the plus and minus signs for two AAs. Not only can you sleep in, you don't even need a functioning alarm clock.

If you'll be taking your grandchildren trick-or-treating at night, you'll want special accessories to keep you safe. Night vision goggles or extra large eyeglasses are a must, which makes a Ghost Buster costume a great choice. A high-powered lantern is also important—one with 360 degree coverage. You can affix it to a hard hat and go as a coal miner. Or mount the lantern in a red wagon, plop in your grandchild costumed as a Dalmation puppy, and dress as Cruella de Vil.

Another option for nighttime protection is the Badass Biker outfit. Start with some hideous false teeth. Then get a heavy chain belt (made from a real chain from a hardware store). Buy a beat up moto jacket (short for motorcycle—I'm so cool) at Savers. Top it off with a generous application of yellow and black police crime scene tape. This should scare off potential muggers along your trick-or-treating route.

Not going outdoors for Halloween? If house parties are more your style, you'll have a wider range of options. Forget about anything from the movie *Frozen*. We're way too old for that. We can, however, go as a modified version of the Ice Bucket Challenge. Begin with a clear plastic shower curtain liner worn as a poncho. Add a standard bucket, but fill it with acrylic cubes. The last thing you need is someone pouring ice cold water on you. Unless you're wearing SpongeBob panties.

For a trendy but affordable costume, create an enormous version of Pharrell Williams' hat. Use one of those huge brown paper bags—the ones you stuff leaves into. Cut openings for your eyes, nose and mouth. Also armholes. Then attach a roll of corrugated paper around the opening at knee level to make a narrow brim. You might want to visit Pharrell's hat on Facebook to be sure you have the proportions right. Yes, his hat has it's own FB page.

Those who are tired of the alarmist responses to the Ebola scare can make a political statement by going as Chicken Little. Take a large bag of poly fluff (the stuffing in throw pillows, aka toss pillows in New England) and glue clumps of it to an old jogging suit. Intersperse these with pieces of blue construction paper, cut into random shapes. As you wander around the Halloween party, shout: *"The sky is falling! The sky is falling!"* as you look up toward the ceiling. Enough said.

Here's a fun idea that retirees can appreciate. Pick up an inexpensive set of doctor's scrubs and dye them orange. Then get a bottle of dark blue ink at an art shop and pour generous amounts on the scrubs at the elbow, upper arms and thigh areas. When guests ask, tell them you're dressed as *"Orange Is the New Black and Blue."* Or maybe: *"Black and Blue Is the New Orange."* Whatever.

As you can see, there are many low-cost and easy-to-create Halloween costumes that make sense for retirees this year. I hope you have fun putting them together, and even more fun wearing them. Be sure to post pictures on your Facebook page.

Manipulating Those
On-Line Ads

Original Post Date Nov. 11, 2014

Now that I'm retired, I'm on my computer and on the Internet more than ever. I'm increasingly aware of the ads that appear in the sidebars of browser windows and in some emails. I've also noticed how the content of these ads changes over time.

In the beginning, we were all getting offers for Viagra, or ones asking if we'd like to enlarge our penis to improve our sex life. These were dumb on so many counts, the most enormous being that more than half of the people seeing them don't have penises. What a colossal waste of advertising money! Over time, the software companies refined their placement algorithms (or whatever tool they use) so that those promotions appear mostly for viewers who have an interest in augmenting their equipment.

It didn't take long for me to realize that the things I surfed about in researching my blog topics started showing up in my sidebars and in the banners at the top of the window. They kept appearing for weeks after I'd looked them up, even though I no longer had any interest in them. What's worse, my initial inquiries were solely for the purpose of the post at hand. I never had any personal plans to wear or buy bow ties, for instance. I just researched all the various styles for a blog entry about their renaissance.

When we moved into our condominium, I purchased a MacBook Air, so I'm on my laptop much of the time. My husband purchased an HP laptop, which turned out to be a lemon. He returned it and decided to rethink what type of device made sense for him. In the meantime, I let him use my desktop computer. He's been spending hours each day searching the Internet for products for his store.

About a week ago, Jagdish replaced his defective laptop, so I'm now on my desktop Mac again much of the time. I can tell which product categories he's been researching by looking at the ads I'm getting. While these are a step above Viagra, they're still for products in which I have no interest. I should probably consider wearing a Fitbit activity band, so I know how lazy I am in my new cocoon. But the ads aren't going to make me buy one, much less become more active.

Likewise, I'm not excited about singing bowls, essential oils and gemstones with "special properties." I must admit, those ads are a step up from the ones for basement storage shelves. They've taken over my laptop ever since I looked up those offerings at Home Depot. But none of these are of interest to me. It dawned on me that they're not even visually attractive.

I decided that I needed to take control of my browser and email screens. I made a list of things that I would enjoy looking at in those sidebars and banners. Things that were graphically exciting or that made me feel all warm and fuzzy. Items like freshwater lakes and paisley prints and perennial flowers of New England. And of course, cats. Then I Googled them. Every time I found a website with photos I liked, I bookmarked the page.

Now I'm fine-tuning the process. For example, *PaisleyPrintBoutique.com* seemed like it would have gorgeous photos, but their homepage is loaded with earrings. Hence, no bookmark. The blog *ThreadsofHistory* probably won't help with my browser ads, but I bookmarked that one anyway. "Musings and tidbits on textile design and creation, from prehistory to the modern day" is SO in my wheelhouse. The author stopped posting in 2010, but there are dozens of entries for me to read when we're snowed in this winter.

Another site mentioned textile print blocks, so I searched on that and turned up some interesting graphics on *woodprintblocks.com* worth bookmarking. This in turn led to block printing, but that was a visual dead end. By now I'm sure you get the idea.

For the process to work effectively, I need to visit each of the sites I've marked just before I shut down my browser each day. That flags those sites as most recent and also as frequently visited, which moves them up in the ad hierarchy. It also puts a smile on my face as I log off. I'm still figuring out how many of my selected sites I need in order to shut out the ads I don't want to see. This plan is, after all, a work in progress.

But that's one of the great things about being retired. At this stage of my life, just about everything is a work in progress. Especially me.

Retirement Sparks Redux

Section V

Labels & Identity

Retirement Terminology—
Group Names

Original Post Date Dec. 15, 2012

A photo in a magazine showed a huge black cloud of birds, high above rooftops. It was described as a 'murmuration of starlings.' I'd heard of a 'gaggle of geese' and an 'exaltation of larks,' but never 'murmuration.' I was entranced and instantly fell in love with the term. A little Googling turned up a 'gulp of swallows,' a 'convocation of eagles,' and — be still my heart — an 'ostentation of peacocks.'

It turns out many of these are poetic inventions, often centuries old, and several books on such terms have been published over the years. The website *WorldWideWords.org* tells us:

> *Type 'collective nouns' into any Web search engine: you'll find dozens of sites featuring them, though the level of wit is sadly variable.*

Upon reading Michael Quinion's article on collective nouns [*http://www.worldwidewords.org/articles/collectives.htm*], I likewise instantly fell in love with his website. I also decided that I have an obligation to come up with some witty 'collective nouns' for retirees and seniors.

Here goes.

Recreational groups:

A gabble of Mah Jong players, gossiping about their neighbors

A sproutation of garden club members, repotting their seedlings

A slithering of shuffleboard addicts, slipping their discs

A procrastination of checkers enthusiasts, plotting their moves

A bouffant of square dancers at the community center hoedown

A muster of dominoes aficionados, lining up their tiles

Some everyday collectives:

A scootation of Hoveround® riders, headed to the mall

A droople of Sansabelt® wearers, hiking up their pants

A tippling of sherry lovers, imbibing in the afternoon

A snooze of nappers, practicing their snores (after sherry hour...)

An explication of crossword puzzle buffs, filling in the blanks

A loopation of Velcro® devotees, adjusting their shoe straps

Medical terms:

A clatter of denture wearers, adjusting their teeth

A glom of seniors on statins, trying to unclog their arteries

A congestion of fiber enthusiasts, on line at the restroom (also trying to unclog...)

A tumble of folks with vertigo, riding the 'down' escalator

A gimp of orthopedic patients, doing physical therapy

Special bunches of women:

A frumple of blue-haired old ladies, crocheting toilet paper cozies

A noblesse of volunteers, dressed in their finest goody two shoes

A swarm of quilters, circling at their weekly bee

A dithering of envelope stuffers, helping with a church mailing

An omnibustle of book club members, arguing about character motivation

There you have it, my list to date. I hope you find the level of wit consistently above average.

Retirement Nicknames

Original Post Date Jan. 26, 2013

Nine-year-old Samantha Gordon weighs roughly 62 pounds and plays football in an otherwise all-boys league in Utah. In 2012 (her first year playing), she racked up 1,911 yards and 35 touchdowns, earning her the nickname 'Sweet Feet.' It's an endearing term, in part because the juxtaposition of 'sweet' with 'feet' is so unexpected. You wouldn't be surprised to hear feet described as 'smelly,' or maybe 'stinky,' but 'sweet' is another story. We've all heard 'sweet cheeks' before. But 'sweet feet'? I don't think so.

You just know where this is headed. My mind is rushing headlong down the track marked: *unexpected nicknames for retirees.* Let's begin with feet, those overburdened extremities that bear the brunt of our weight gains (along with our knees). Those appendages prone to bunions and corns and hammertoes. All of which can lead to **'orthopedic feet.'** As the saying goes (or not): *If the shoe doesn't fit, wear it.* (The moniker, that is.)

Moving on to other appendages, the retired ballroom dancer who refuses to give up competitions is no longer known as 'twinkle toes.' She's grown her toenails long and filed them into weaponry that peeks out of her dancing sandals. Most weeks, her nails are actually longer than her heels are high. This has earned her a new title: **'stiletto toes.'**

And while we're on the subject of digits, most of you will have heard the phrase 'dowager's hump.' Our list includes '**dowager's pinky**.' That's what we've dubbed the bent over old lady with the crooked fingers, especially the little one that she sticks out when she's having her afternoon tea. I am too cruel today.

Another unexpected name tied to physical attributes is the retiree's equivalent of 'freckle face.' We're now dealing with liver spots, not freckles and we've christened her '**Pleiades**.' That's the seven sisters constellation (like the seven spectacular age spots on her left cheek), and the website earthsky.org tells us it's "visible from virtually every place that humanity inhabits Earth's globe." That's pretty much true of her liver spots, too.

Moving ever so slightly away from cheeks, we come to our next nickname. You've probably heard of the 'fuzzy navel,' my late mother's favorite cocktail. Well, we have a retired gentleman whose ear hair has grown so long he's known affectionately as '**fuzzy earlobes**.' I bet you're tickled to read this one.

Staying in this general vicinity, and keeping in mind that U.S. Marines are called 'leathernecks,' let me introduce you to '**jello neck**.' I don't think I have to tell you how that sobriquet came about. (Lexicography buffs: there's a *double entendre* in that last sentence.)

This option fits into no particular category. Can you guess the origin of the endearing label '**Rice Krispies**'? It's how we describe the retiree whose bodily noises have now reached the point where he goes snap, crackle and pop, even when he's sitting still. My bad. Forgive me.

Moving on to some names that came about because of certain clothing. First we have '**shiny butt**.' He insists on wearing the same corduroy pants even when the behind has been worn down to zero nap. Then there's the retired gentleman who never leaves his house without some dapper hat covering his bald spot. It's usually a fedora, so a tip of the lid to '**beau brimmel**.'

We can't leave this group without mentioning the older women who let their hosiery (especially trouser socks) collapse onto their ankles in nylon puddles. I'm labeling them '**ankle rolls**,' but I just know there's a cleverer pet name for them if we noodle it for awhile. And speaking of older women, let's not forget the nosey rumor mongers in our neighborhoods. We'll refer to them as '**gossip laureates**' and hope the sarcasm doesn't elude them.

Finally, we have a nickname many of us can claim. It's for those who have not one, not two, but at least three (and maybe four) different prescriptions for various eyeglass needs. When they're merged into one pair of glasses (avoiding the entanglement of multiple leashes), they yield lenses that give the wearer a most peculiar appearance. Ever wonder what happened to the "girl with kaleidoscope eyes" in the Beatle's song, *Lucy in the Sky with Diamonds*? Well, she retired and became '**prism eyes**.'

There you have it. A basketful of nicknames, pet names, monikers, sobriquets, roses by a lot of other names, for the retirees in your life. I fully expect to have several of them leveled at my husband and me when we walk together. I can hear people whispering: *"There go shiny butt and ankle rolls."* At least they didn't mention my jello neck.

The Search for Exclusivity

Original Post Date Jul. 20, 2013

I read somewhere (probably in *Ad Age*) that the makers of Grey Poupon mustard screen people who want to friend them on Facebook. If you don't cut the mustard (sorry, couldn't help myself), they ignore you. Apparently it's all part of their marketing strategy to position themselves as the mustard for the upper crust. (Again, sorry.)

This gave me an idea. What if I announced that I'm screening people who want to follow my blog? Although quite a few of you read the blog, only a handful signed on as followers. Perhaps if I became more exclusive, it would give me cachet. Cachet usually leads to a following.

This seemed like a good plan, until I started thinking about how I would screen folks. I took a closer look at Grey Poupon, expecting it to become my paragon for screening. Here's what I uncovered on their Facebook page.

GREY POUPON was founded in 1777 and... is generally regarded as the classiest condiment in the world. Their page had 64,309 "likes." There was no apparent screening mechanism. Perhaps the *Ad Age* article drew so much attention they couldn't handle the volume, so they opened the floodgates and let everybody in.

The "General Information" link gave a soupçon of this. Their "Rules of the Road" has four paragraphs and five bullet points wherein they: *"...tip our hats to those who create a civilized community... where fans can share their passion for GREY POUPON mustard..."* And so on, including legalese about giving them the unrestricted right to use whatever you post.

The final paragraph states: *"For existing fans: if you do not wish to be a fan of the official GREY POUPON page... please feel free to "unlike" our page."* "Aha!" said I. They DID have a different mindset when they created their Facebook page. Those existing, prescreened fans were more "civilized" and likely to be put off by the hoi polloi allowed to post on the site now. This did not help me with my own screening, so I needed to move on.

Before I did, I took a gander at the historical list of commercials. I stayed just long enough to determine that the person who edits their Facebook page doesn't know how to spell "rakish." I would have clued them in to this error, but you need to "like" the page before you can post on it. There's no way I'm engaging with hoi polloi who could never pass muster, much less mustard (from a Volkswagon Beetle window).

Back to my own screening criteria. Here are some things I feel I have a right to expect from my blog followers. They should know how to spell "rakish" and they should look good in a hat set at a rakish angle. They should be able to tell the difference between hoi polloi and swells at a distance of 100 feet, which means they need to know what a "swell" looks like.

I'd like them to know how to make a kickin' pot of vegetarian chili and to be able to say "thank you" in at least one language other than English. They should have a stash of those recyclable grocery bags in the trunk of their car. They don't talk in a loud voice on their cell phone when they're in public, and they know when (and how) to turn it off. They brake for animals; they do NOT speed up.

Conversely, here are some deal breakers. Have you ever caught a fish with your bare hands? Collected empty beer cans to make a piece of furniture? Do you have more than three tattoos? Are any of them larger than 4" across? Would you look right at home in a WalMart? Even if that Walmart were in Alabama or Mississippi? (*Especially* if it's in Alabama or Mississippi?) I don't have to tell you what a "yes" to any of these means.

Finally, here are a few multiple-choice questions to test your suitability to follow me.

1. Which of the following do you consider a culinary treat?
   a) Ahi sashimi
   b) Squirrel stew
   c) Eggplant rollatini

2. Your window box garden is now growing:
   a) Fresh basil
   b) Weeds
   c) Weed

3. Your favorite summer footwear is:
   a) Merrell or Teva sandals
   b) (For men) Tube socks and Birkenstocks; (for women) flip-flops
   c) Tennies or boat shoes

If you answered any letter b, you're too *déclassé*; don't even apply. If you answered any letter c, I'll put you on my waiting list, but don't hold your breath (and don't inhale…). The rest of you can fill out my screener online. Be sure to attach a photo of you in a hat set at a rakish angle.

It Seems I Might Be A Tomato

Original Post Date Aug. 17, 2013

The New York Times ran an article about how vegetables have their own seasons within the usual four that we think of. The article's author, Melissa Clark, called it "microseasonality." Apparently, each vegetable (and fruit, I assume) has it's own microseasonal schedule. What especially caught my eye was the evocative language Clark used to describe a tomato's seasons. It was eerily familiar. Simply put, it seems as though I might be a tomato.

We're all used to hearing the stages of our lives compared to the seasons of the year. You have the Spring of your youth, your Summer salad days, the maturing Fall of your life and the Winter (of your discontent?) Vegetables can go through all their mircoseasons within one traditional calendar season. Clark's explanation of the tomato's progress explained it in a way we can all understand.

They start out "hard and green and mildly acidic." Could she be describing the "me" of my youth with any more accuracy? People who knew me well back then used to say that I had brass... Well, you get the idea. And in my youth, I was as green as those little apples that God didn't make. As with many young people, I thought I knew everything, but in fact I knew almost nothing. Or at least, nothing of value.

Like the tomato, I probably reached "peak ripeness" mid-season in my life. That's when I was the most successful in my career (and financially), though at the time, I expected far greater "success" in the years over the horizon. Silly me. It wasn't until later on in my personal microseasons that I realized there are so many ways to define one's own success. And so few of them involve money.

Also like the tomato, the late-season me became "overripe and overly soft." I mellowed with age and many would likewise credit me with "gaining sweetness," especially compared to my acidic youth. One look in the mirror also confirmed that I was "losing texture," unless you count wrinkles as texture, which I don't. How much more in sync with the tomato could my microseasons be?

I'll tell you how much more. Clark described tomatoes at the end of the growing season as: "...back to green, not ripening fully before" (horrors) "falling off the vine." Indeed. In the winter of my microseason I'm realizing that there's so very much I don't know. So much I will never know, even if I reach my nineties before I fall off the vine.

But Clark reserved the most apt description for last. She said that the "later-season specimen... has had a chance to grow fatter. The flesh gets flabby, the seeds larger and more distracting."

Seriously. Is she describing a tomato? Or is she talking about my neck wattle, my wing flaps and my age spots? While I'm comforted to learn that even late-season tomatoes have usefulness, I don't look forward to becoming pickled or fried. I'm also not anxious to have my "spongy core" cut out.

I prefer to think of myself as aging into a piquant salsa. Or better yet, sliced onto a panini under some locally-made buffalo mozzarella. Drizzled with extra virgin olive oil and garnished with fresh basil. And served with (what else?) a nice bottle of *Chianti Classico*. Put me in that scenario, and I'll be content to fall off the vine any time Mother Nature calls me.

Crazy Holidays for Retirees

Original Post Date Sep. 21, 2013

Kelly Ripa announced on *Live with Kelly and Michael* that September 9 was National Hermit Crab Awareness Day. Until that moment, I wasn't aware of this holiday. I felt like the woman in the Prego commercial who is surprised to learn she prefers that brand to the one she's been buying for years. An audio thought bubble opines: "I wonder what other questionable choices I've made..." And she flashes back to show how she's picked nerdy-looking men, or horrific hairstyles, or too-trendy clothes.

My thought bubble read: "I wonder what crazy holidays for retirees I've been missing out on..." After all, some restaurants give you a free dessert on your birthday. Who knows what exclusive treatment could be available for retirees on holidays that are off our radar? You'll be happy to learn that I've researched this and I'm sharing some special days with you, in calendar order.

Dowager's Hump Awareness Day occurs the second Wednesday of each month. People who are still working get to celebrate Hump Day every week. All the dowagers get is one day a month. We're still researching appropriate ways to celebrate this holiday. For starters, skip the camel jokes altogether, no matter how cute you think that GEICO commercial is. Free pudding at all restaurants would be a nice touch. It seldom has any lumps, much less humps.

National Mismatched Plaid Day coincides with St. Patrick's Day. Many people wear plaid for that holiday, Lord only knows why. It's the Scots who make a big deal of displaying the plaid of their clan's heritage, not the Irish. No matter. Retirees who wear mismatched plaids on this holiday get free beer at any bar with a name starting with "O." Which is to say, there's free beer at virtually every Irish pub for retirees who wear plaid, period. Older folks never do plaid right.

Be still my heart! There's an entire week set aside to celebrate *Quaint Expressions* (like *"Be still my heart..."*) It begins the third Sunday in April, with *Cat's Pajamas Day* (my favorite expression of the group). Retirees get to stay in their jammies all day, even if they go out to eat. And not just for brunch, for any meal. You can check out the rest of the week (including free honey on *The Bee's Knees Wednesday*) on line.

National Velcro Appreciation Days are June 19 and September 13. This invention is so fabulous that it's celebrated twice a year: first on the birthday of the inventor (George de Mestral) and then on the day he filed the original patent. We commemorate these happiest of retirees' holidays by giving them a 20% discount on any article of clothing or household item that uses hook-and-loop fasteners (Velcro is a trademark) in any way whatsoever.

After a long battle, *National Nap Appreciation Day* was declared to be the summer solstice, June 20 or 21. Check your Farmers' Almanac each year. The competing faction wanted the winter solstice, December 21 or 22, the day with the most darkness. June aficionados won out. How can you expect retirees to get through about 15 hours of daylight without a late-afternoon nap? Retirees get to take a snooze wherever they are that afternoon. This includes in the driver's seat of their car, at a stoplight.

National Cranky Pants Day is celebrated the Monday after Thanksgiving. We're all in a lousy mood by then, even if we didn't fight crowds to get some early holiday shopping done. We were probably stuck in traffic, or in a line some-place we had no choice but to go at some point that weekend. You might think this holiday should be for everyone, not just retirees, but it's not. We've earned the right to be cranky. Others haven't. Give us a wide berth on Cranky Pants Day.

Medicare Post-Enrollment Exhalation Day happens every fall, the day after the deadline to enroll in or change retirement healthcare plans. As an added stress, it can move from year to year, but it's often December 7. If you're not sure when it is, listen for the collective whoosh of retirees sighing in relief that the deadline has once again passed. On this day, retirees get to cut in line at the pharmacy. Come to think of it, let them cut in line wherever they are. Or else be prepared to listen to all their ailments.

No doubt there are other holidays well-suited to being celebrated by retirees, but these are the first seven that I turned up. Be sure to take some time to observe every one of them in a memorable way. If you're not retired yet, do something appropriate on each of the days for someone who is. A blogger friend, perhaps? Just sayin'…

Fraternal Organizations
for Retirees
Original Post Date Sep. 28, 2013

In high school, I desperately wanted to be a cheerleader. Desperate is the operative word; I couldn't execute a proper cartwheel, much less do a full split. I wound up in the marching band, where I made many good friends, several of whom I'm still in touch with. I didn't join the band in college, though I considered it. I was too busy keeping my head (and grades) above water. I had no interest in sororities; the cheerleading failure probably scarred me for life.

I mention this because my once guilty pleasure, *The View*, briefly discussed sororities and fraternities in one of its Hot Topics segments. One faction liked that you could travel the country and be welcomed by sisters (or brothers) from other chapters as one of their own. Another faction decried that the very concept of a fraternal organization was based on the notion of exclusivity and, by extension, exclusion.

Suddenly I had one of my flashes of inspiration: there should be fraternal organizations especially for retirees. Ones like *Tappa Kegga Beer*, but geared to the interests of folks our age. Naturally, I set to work identifying suitable candidates. Organizations that would be welcoming, inclusionary and not exclusionary. Organizations with catchy names that could be screen printed on bowling-shirts and embroidered on canvas tote bags.

Say for instance, *Takea Nappa Day*, the senior snooze fraternity. It's unisex, so both men and women can join. The initiation rites include a mid-afternoon nap that must last at least 20 minutes, but not more than two hours. There isn't a retiree out there who should have a problem meeting that requirement.

There are three sororities for those who might consider joining a garden club. There's *Planta Lotta Flora*, and it's sister sororities *Weeda Bita Day* and *Oma Achin Back*. Some chapters of this last one don't even require you to have a garden. Talk about being inclusionary!

Retirees generally find that they have a lot more time to engage in sports and other physical activity. There are a number of fraternal groups for active types. Those who practice the minimum of exertion may want to join *Walka Milea Day*. For the slightly more strenuous, there's the sorority *Yoga Cobra Dog*, or *Yo Co Do* for short. And for seniors who are into truly challenging exercise, we have the senior crew fraternity, *Rho Grampa Rho*.

Some of the organizations draw their members based on what they wear. Chief among these is *Polli Esta Slax*. Sisters and brothers take an oath to never wear pants made out of natural fibers. One of the hazing rituals involves a blindfolded test wherein the pledges must feel six pieces of fabric and decide: polyester or natural fiber? Get more than two of them wrong, and you're out. Or rather, not in.

One of the fraternities I uncovered caters to men who feature themselves to be what my mother would have called "dandies." Eligibility includes always being impeccably dressed, with hair combed perfectly and wearing far too much cologne. If you know someone who believes more is not enough, suggest that he join *Spritza Bita Aftashave*.

If you have at least three grandchildren, consider pledging *Nana Bragsa Lot*. You'll need to have a smartphone with a top of the line photo sharing app. Chances are one of your progeny has already provided you with this, the better to see their own offspring.

Finally, some fraternal organizations celebrate the riches that a well-planned retirement affords the retiree. There's the self-explanatory *Gotta Primo Condo*, which has a high concentration of membership in Florida, North and South Carolina and Arizona. And there's the equally self-explanatory *Takea Trippa Year*. It's membership is concentrated in metro areas around major universities.

Finding it hard to choose among all these exciting prospects? Don't worry. They're so non-exclusionary that—unlike typical fraternities and sororities—you can join more than one. I'm just glad none of them requires members to do a cartwheel or a split.

Designer Dogs
for Retirees

Original Post Date Sep. 27, 2014

I recently noted that virtually all the canine pets in our condo development are small breeds. I'm not sure why. Our association doesn't cap the allowable weight of pets, only the number (two). But some communities limit dogs to 30 pounds. On the heels of this finding, I noticed that *Time* magazine included a feature on designer dogs in its "The Answers Issue." This confluence of tidbits unleashed the idea for this post.

Since many retirees live where pet weight is regulated, I've included a number of smaller creatures in my collection. Read the details of each designer breed to find the perfect one for your needs.

New members of a condo community may want a dog that conveys status. The best choice for a high-end symbol is the *LhaChiDa*—a blend of Lhasa Apso and Chihuahua, with just a hint of Dalmation in the lineage. The Dal parent harks back several generations, assuring that the LhaChiDa will not get too large and will have only small and occasional (not too) black spots. As Chris Farley aka Matt Foley used to say on *Saturday Night Live*: "Well, la-dee-frickin-da."

Speaking of Farley, those who have packed on the pounds since they stopped going to work should consider a *Porkie*.

This Pug—Yorkshire Terrier crossbreed is so chubby that just looking at it will provide incentive for you to exercise daily. A word of caution: the Porkie may want to join you on your daily walks. If it loses too much weight, it will begin to look like a Shar-Pei. Ditto for its owners.

Retirees generally make frequent doctors visits, where they're likely to spend considerable time in the waiting room. The perfect dog to tuck into your medical tote for company is the *Dachsador*. This Dachshund—Labrador mix loves going to the doctor's office. It's sized like the Dachshund, but it's as devoted as the Lab. And please don't send me any jokes about lab tests. Or cat scans.

For older women who have become dependent on weekly appointments at the beautician, we recommend the *Pompador*. This cross between a Pomeranian and a Labrador has the size and pouf of its smaller mother and the temperament of its larger father. Note that if you cross a male Pomeranian with a female Labrador you get a Labramanian. These dogs are used to search for truffles in certain Balkan countries.

While we're on the subject of hair, a designer dog for those who are going bald is the *TerPei*. This Terrier—Shar-Pei mix has been bred to perch comfortably on top of your head when you leave home. Sometimes affectionately called the Terpe, this wonderful little guy will happily drape on top of you like a small rug. Your friends and neighbors will have no idea how thin your own hair has become underneath all his wrinkles.

Retirees are prone to bragging about their grandchildren, often exaggerating their achievements and talents. We have two breeds especially for them. The first is the *Malorkie*, a Maltese—Yorkshire Terrier blend. This is the choice for grandparents who embellish only slightly about their progeny. The second is the *BullShitz*, a Bulldog—Shih Tzu crossbreed. This is the go-to option for those who fabricate outright the successes of their grandkids, who of course have zero shortcomings.

If you've moved into a community where you're worried about your neighbors snooping, consider getting a *SharpShooTer* to guard your homestead. This breed has a pair of designer parents: a Shar Pei/Shih Tzu mix on its mother's side, and a Poodle/Terrier union on its father's. It looks like a cute little thing, so it lures snoopers into a false sense of security as they lurk in your bushes. Then the yappy, manic influence of its father emerges, startling the intruder into a frantic retreat.

For retirees who are addicted to catalog shopping, the *Speagle* will be a valuable companion. This Spaniel—Beagle cross is a true hunting dog. It has a storied history of helping its owners find obscure products by sniffing through hundreds of pages in just minutes. You can generally adopt a Speagle online.

Finally, the perfect designer dog for retirees who have discovered the joys of napping is the *Schnoozer*. This Schnauzer—Poodle creation is at home lying on any soft horizontal surface. As long as you have room for this mid-sized pet, you'll have company on your afternoon nap no matter where you decide to take it. If you live in a small condominium, you might want to opt for the sub-breed, the MiniSchnoozer. It's a cross between a Miniature Schnauzer and a Toy Poodle. And no, it doesn't take catnaps.

There you have it. Ten designer dogs created especially for retirees. I'm here to serve.

Nicknames for Senior Body Parts

Original Post Date Oct. 18, 2014

I recently heard that Shonda Rhimes coined the word "vajayjay" as a nickname for vagina because network censors wouldn't let her use the anatomical label in scripts for her hit TV show, *Grey's Anatomy*. Then I caught *The View's* Rosie Perez using "hooha," also a popular nickname for... well, you know. It occurred to me that as seniors, retirees need to come up with alternative names for certain of our body parts and ailments. The ones whose real names somewhat awkwardly describe... well, you know that, too.

I've put together a starter list especially for my readers. The official names are shown first, then the slang. I've also provided a sentence or two using the nickname and/or elaborating on it. I hope you find these colorful terms useful in your conversations with family, friends and physicians.

Bunion — *Booya*
"The older I get, the more uncomfortable my booya gets. Pretty soon I'll need a booyectomy." Good luck getting your insurance company to cover the procedure. Booya!

Neck Wattle — *Natty*
"I'm going to start wearing bow ties to obscure my natty." But of course. Isn't that what every well-dressed gentleman wears for his GQ spread?

Droopy Ear Lobes — *Doobies*
"I can't wear dangly earrings anymore now that my doobies have gotten so long." Do not confuse this with something you smoke.

Belly Pooch — *Boochy*
"My boochy is bigger than a bread box." And a related term:
Saggy Abdomen — *Sabdo*
"If I don't do sit-ups every morning, I get a sabdo."
If you have a boochy or a sabdo, and especially if your boochy morphs into a sabdo, it's time for Spanx.

Fallen Arches — *Floppers*
"As I've gotten older, my feet have developed major floppers." I feel your pain. My floppers have absolutely no cushioning anymore. I feel like I'm walking on concrete all the time.

Flatulence — *The Flappies*
"When I eat raw mushrooms, I get the flappies. It's even worse when I eat a lot of beans." Stay away from campfires! (Remember *Blazing Saddles?*)

Hemorrhoids/Polyps — *The Pollies*
"Now that football season is here, I need to eat more fiber. There's nothing worse than the pollies when you're in those rock hard nosebleed seats at a game." Two words: inflatable inner-tube.

Dowager's/Widow's Hump — *Doho*
"I'm paying special attention to my posture so I don't develop a doho." This is particularly important for those who

have *opo* (osteoporosis), because really bad opo can lead to a doho. Then every day is Hump Day. Oh, no!

And my favorite slang term:
Bristly Goat Hairs (on chin) — *Stiffies*
"It's bad enough that I have fuzzy sideburns, but I also have stiffies on my chin." And after a few glasses of wine, I have fizzies and stuffies.

I could go on, but sometimes too much of a good thing is overkill. No doubt you can come up with a few nicknames of your own. The only guideline is this: if it sounds better than the anatomical term, it's a keeper. Happy slanging!

Retirement Sparks Redux

Section VI

Science & Technology

Retirement Sparks Redux

Things Robots Should Not Do

Original Post Date Mar. 9, 2013

Technology advances so rapidly and so pervasively that it's a challenge for retirees to keep up. One example: robots are increasingly common in our lives, often in ways we aren't aware of. I'm on board with letting these unmanned machines do more for us, especially mundane chores such as vacuuming and cleaning the litter box (as long as the cat isn't in it). But there are some things that, in my opinion, they just should not do.

A *New York Times* article questioned robotic hysterectomies, based in part on a report in *The Journal of the American Medical Association*. Upon closer reading, I learned the article wasn't so much questioning the use of robots to perform hysterectomies. It was noting that the outcomes were not more favorable than for laparoscopic ones, and therefore didn't justify the considerable extra cost.

The last item on my list of things I'd welcome having a robot do is my hysterectomy. This got me thinking: What other procedures or chores would I not want to entrust to a pile of nuts, bolts, solenoids and sensors (or whatever stuff bots are made of)? It didn't take me long to come up with a sizable list.

There's no way I'd let an android clean out my earwax. For sure, I'd wind up looking like someone from a Steve Martin skit, but with a cotton swab sticking out from each side of my head instead of an arrow. Likewise, I would not recommend letting mechanical grabbers try to retrieve bellybutton lint. Well, not if you're an innie anyway. The outies can decide for themselves.

Along similar lines, I really can't picture a bot flossing my teeth. With all my caps and fillings, I have so many cracks and crevices that I have trouble getting around in my own mouth. A robo-flosser would surely get tied up in knots. I can see it running amok, trying to untangle its pincers, digging its back claws into my tongue. No thank you. I'll keep doing my own flossing and my dental hygienist will keep thanking me for it.

My eyesight gets worse each year, making me feel like I'm becoming my mother. There's an entire post in there somewhere, but right now I'm reminded that she had me do her eye makeup when she was older. She found it difficult to navigate the narrow space between her glasses and her eyelids, especially since everything is backwards in a mirror. If I wore eye shadow, I might let an android apply that. But there's no way I'd let it put on mascara. I'm a blinker and I'd have raccoon eyes for certain.

Moving into a different arena, you'd have to be crazy to let some bionic dude fill out your Medicare forms. Or any health-related or government paperwork for that matter. You can bet that the software controlling it would get hacked by the Chinese or by a former Starbucks employee. Next thing you know, you're thrown in jail—or committed to a mental hospital—while your assets are drained into an offshore account.

We've been hearing a lot about drones lately. When an Alitalia pilot reported seeing a small, black one below his plane as he was approaching JFK airport, the story hardly made a blip on the news. I thought a drone like that could be a good way to wash my upstairs windows. Then I remembered Google Earth's cameras. It's unnerving to think what a window-washing snoop might photograph once it removed the grime.

I suppose I could let a robot tidy up my sock drawer, but it would take a lot of programming to replicate the logic behind how I organize colors. It hardly seems worth the effort. When you consider all the downsides, there aren't many things automatons should do in our daily lives. And there are plenty of things they most definitely should *not* do. Writing my blog is one of them. An electronic clone wouldn't have my charm, my wit, my humor, my (fill in the blank).

I might trust one to open a bottle of wine for me once my post was written; but with my luck, the doppelganger would share my appreciation for the grape. The wine rack would be empty before I knew it. The drunken bot would be careening around the house, corkscrew in claw, bumping into furniture and scaring the cat out of eight of his lives.

No. That's one more thing robots should not do. I'll open my wine myself. On that note…

Why We Forget More As We Age

Original Post Date Jul. 13, 2013

Recently I discovered a scientific basis for why we forget so much as we get older. To explain this, I need to put it in biological context. A woman is born with a finite number of eggs in her ovaries. Once they've all made that monthly journey down her fallopian tubes (or have shriveled up *in situ*), there are no more eggs to be had.

It's much the same with brain cells wired for memory. Our brains have a finite capacity for the number of things we can remember. Once our hippocampus is full (usually as we approach retirement age), there's no more room for new stuff. Depending on your sentiments and the type of brain you have, you either fail to store any new information, or the new information bumps out something older that's already in there.

If you're paying attention, you're no doubt wondering how your gray matter decides whether to refuse to remember new information vs. getting rid of something older, and what that "something older" might be. A key factor is the state of the economy when you reach your golden years.

Accountants will be familiar with two ways to value inventory: LIFO (Last In, First Out) and FIFO (First In, First Out). In an inflationary economy, companies often prefer

LIFO accounting (unless they're highly profit-driven). Inventory used up is valued at the higher cost of a recent purchase, not the lower cost of something procured years earlier. So it looks like less cash is tied up in inventory. (BTW companies can't just switch back and forth willy nilly.)

An older brain will simply refuse to remember something new unless it's really important. In that case, in a deflationary economy (speaking hypothetically, of course), a FIFO brain jettisons the oldest memories first, if it can find them. A LIFO-economy brain bumps out one of the more recently-acquired pieces of information. This explains why, in the real world, those with failing memories can often recall things from decades past, but not from yesterday.

Like everything else involved with gray matter, this is not a simple, clear-cut process. There's a certain amount of emotion involved, too. If the positive emotional value of the memory about to be expunged is at least twice that of the new item, the brain will refuse the new information. Similarly, if the negative baggage of the old stuff is twice that of the incoming, it's out with the old, in with the new. I hope you're getting all of this.

If you're of a certain age, expect to be forgetting more and more recent knowledge from now on. Baby Boomers have little chance of approaching retirement in a deflationary economy. Interest rates may start ratcheting up next year. If rates go up, can inflation (and LIFO memory) be far behind?

Getting back to the ovary/eggs comparison. Scientific advancements enable a woman to use a donor egg to create a baby. We need to co-opt that science for gray matter in order to counteract the forgetfulness that comes with aging. We donate blood. We donate bone marrow. Is it too much to ask to be able to donate a few cells from one hippocampus to another?

While we wait for this breakthrough, there are certain mental exercises you can do to help you retain the memories you cherish most. If you were paying attention three paragraphs back (and if you're not functioning in extreme LIFO mode), you'll remember that emotions can influence which older memories get expunged to make way for new ones. This tidbit is the basis for your exercises.

Decide which memories you are determined to hold onto. Pair them with some positive emotional imagery. Focus on this pairing for at least two minutes. The emotional connection will now override the LIFO/FIFO functioning of your brain. The memories you want to keep will remain, regardless of where they are in the LIFO/FIFO hierarchy.

Conversely, think of something you're perfectly willing to forget. Pair it with something repulsive in your emotional repertoire. Focus on this pairing for at least four minutes; (bad stuff takes twice as long to jettison). The emotional connection will similarly override the hierarchy.

There you have it. A simple explanation for why we forget more as we age and easy-to-perform exercises to manage this problem while we await a scientific breakthrough to allow brain cell transplants.

In the meantime, it's a good idea to scatter some notebooks around your house and in your car. And several pens or pencils. Write down anything really important, and then hope you don't forget where you put the notebook. You can thank me later, if you remember.

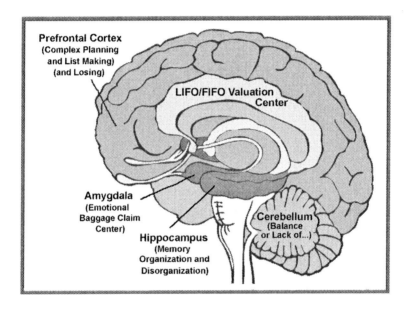

3-D Printers for Retirees

Original Post Date Oct. 12, 2013

News items and crime shows have made me aware of a wide range of products that can be fabricated with the new 3-D printers. It's no surprise that bad guys use them to make guns. But printed pizza? You've got to be kidding me.

Apparently not. Guns. Architectural models. Jewelry. Clothing. And now pizza. The University of Exeter in the UK and US-based 3-D Systems are each working on printing chocolate. (There is a god!) Nike and New Balance already print custom-fit shoes for athletes. A textile company in Pakistan has printed a nylon bikini. It looks a tad like one I crocheted for myself back in the seventies. I hope it holds up in water better than the one I made.

There may be no end to the 3-D printing possibilities, but there can certainly be a beginning, and I'm here to provide it. A 3-D printer could be a retiree's new best friend.

How about walking shoes with Velcro straps? Design them especially to fit your feet, with all their bumps and idio-syncrasies. When the Velcro wears out, print new straps. Have your arches fallen a tad since you made the shoes? Adjust the printer to fit your new curvature (or lack thereof) and make custom insoles. If the shoes lose their grip, make new bottoms. At the rate I've been (not) walking, sole wear-down would be the last of my concerns.

A helpful capability would be printing new lids for Tupperware-type containers. Doesn't every household have an infinite supply of bottoms with missing tops? And a considerable number of tops that match none of those bottoms? This new tool could remove that find-a-match stress from retired life.

Lost a button on your shirt and can't find one with the right diameter and number of holes in your button box? Just print a replacement. This works great for shank buttons, too. You'll still have to sew it on yourself, but getting the right button is half the battle. Actually, getting my husband to tell me he's missing a button is a bigger issue. In our household, laundry day is also discovery day.

The latest 3-D printing use—pizza—opens the door to a whole new category—food. This can take the pressure off us on making a thorough shopping list. You forgot to get romaine? No problem. Simply print up a head. Better yet, print up a few leaves each time you need them. That way they'll always be fresh and crisp. Leaves too thick for you to chew with your late-life teeth? Re-calibrate and print them thinner.

Even better: make yourself new teeth that cut more easily. At the International Dental Show in Cologne, *3Dprintinginsider.com* reported on a German company's process for producing removable partial dentures with these printers. "Data created by intraoral scanners or from scanning an impression" creates a virtual model that is sliced and then directs a "focused laser beam to fuse metal powder in successive layers until the prosthesis is complete." Isn't technology grand!

A truly useful option would be printing new fashion eyewear frames. I don't know about you, but I go through several pairs of magnifiers each month. They're not expensive, but it's hard to find my number. The lenses are generally still OK, but the frames break. If I could print new frames, I could pop in the lenses from the old ones and I'd be in business. Maybe literally, as well as figuratively. Frames-on-demand could make me extremely popular in my retirement community.

Worried that you can't afford a 3-D printer? Get your condo association or one of your activities clubs to buy it. When you have a group in on the purchase, you spread the cost around. There's bound to be enough 3-D printing requests to justify the expense. For starters, you'll be able to print the pizza for your Friday night get-togethers. Or bikinis for lounging around the club's pool. On second thought, maybe not bikinis.

Suddenly I have one of my flashes of genius. Let's get 3-D printers that clone themselves! Then every retiree will be able to afford his own. I hope it's not too long before they figure out how to print a glass of wine.

Epsom Salt—Miracle Cure?

Original Post Date Dec. 7, 2013

A friend emailed me a link to an article on the benefits of Epsom salt. This friend is big on alternative remedies; she also loves the Tea Party, so her endorsements are subject to scrutiny. Some people will not see using "alternative remedies" and "Tea Party" in the same sentence as an oxymoron. I would not be one of them. However, the "9 Reasons To Use Epsom Salt" intrigued me, so I clicked through to *TheAlternativeDaily.com*.

First, they tell us: "Epsom salt is a mineral compound comprised of magnesium and sulfate... used for centuries as a natural remedy for a number of ailments." My attention is waning, but I keep reading about this supposed miracle cure.

The site claims: "Both magnesium and sulfate are readily absorbed into the skin which makes the health benefits readily accessible. Over 325 enzymes in the body are regulated by magnesium... Sulfates improve the rate at which nutrients are absorbed and help to flush out toxins."

I'm surprised that there are 325 enzymes in our bodies, period, much less ones that pay attention to magnesium. The site *http://genomebiology.com* explains that "622 of the (human) enzymes are assigned roles in 135 predicted metabolic pathways... (which) closely match the known nutritional requirements of humans." Of course they do.

I Google "Uses for Epsom Salt," turning up another website, *http://www.saltworks.us*, which has either directly quoted *TheAlternativeDaily.com* or has been plagiarized by the latter, in either case with no attribution. Since I don't know which is the chicken here and which the egg, consider both sites as my sources. I should research this further (Is there a third, primary source?), but I want to get to all those uses.

Most websites group these into Health, Beauty and Home and Garden. Let's start with Health, where there are a number of conditions that should prompt retirees to add Epsom salt to their shopping lists.

If you're stressed (and what retiree isn't), you could be deficient in magnesium. (Or, you could just be experiencing a normal retirement.) *TheAlternativeDaily.com* claims that "magnesium helps the body produce serotonin... a mood elevating chemical..." Call me a skeptic, but doesn't a long soak in a tubful of Crabtree and Evelyn product do the same?

Got muscle pain? Again, what retiree doesn't, at least occasionally? *TheAlternativeDaily.com* tells us: "The sulphates in Epsom salt draw heavy metals and other toxins from cells which can ease muscle pain." *Saltworks.us* credits an Epsom salt soak with treating toenail fungus and easing gout—other senior plagues.

The last Health benefit is the relief of constipation. An empty container I have says take 2 teaspoons in water for a laxative effect, 4 for a cathartic. (That's what Californians call a cleanse.) For those snickering about why I have Epsom salt, it was a yard sale find. I like the pink and black package graphics. It pre-dates zip codes, so it's a collectible.

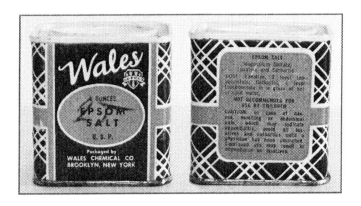

Moving on to Beauty. We're told to use Epsom salt as an "exfoliating facial cleanser" by mixing it with coconut oil and rubbing it on our faces. It also serves as a "hair volumizer," addressing that bane of senior women—thinning hair. This requires warming it in a pan with an equal amount of "deep conditioner," then working it into the hair and leaving it on for 20 minutes.

Finally, let's look at Home and Garden. The use that immediately catches my eye is for cleaning bathroom tiles. Mix "equal parts of Epsom salt with liquid dish detergent. Scrub tiles with the mixture and rinse well." After reading this, I have two thoughts: Who would use the same product to cleanse their face as they use to clean tile grout? And then: Is it the Epsom salt doing this good stuff, or the coconut oil, the conditioner and the detergent?

Full disclosure: my research turned up a Canadian website, *http://saveyourself.ca*, that put the lie to virtually all the purported benefits of Epsom salt. The author, Paul Ingraham, could find scientifically-proven support for only one benefit: easing constipation, an internal use of the salts. He trashes all the external uses.

Ingraham claims that our "skin is almost completely water-proof." I have two comments on that. First, we all know that "almost" doesn't count. Second, tell it to the pharmaceutical companies that market patches for the transdermal delivery of drugs. Also to the makers of the caffeine-infused panties I blogged about awhile ago.

Perhaps the most significant use for Epsom salt is as the inspiration for this *Retirement Sparks* blog post. On that note, I'm off to soak in the tub. But I'll be filling mine with La Source body wash. I'll also have a nice glass of *vino* by my side. Now that's what I call a miracle cure.

Redefining GMOs

Original Post Date Jan. 1, 2014

When General Mills announced that it is changing the production of its original Cheerios to eliminate all Genetically Modified Organisms, it propelled GMOs into the forefront of health controversies in the U.S.

GMOs are biological entities that have been tinkered with scientifically to enhance growth, spur resistance to disease, or otherwise improve the viable yield of crops. DNA material that has been genetically altered is inserted into these organisms with the approval of the FDA.

Newsflash! The GMOs that we really need are Geriatrically Modified Organisms—ones tweaked to maximize compatibility with the constitutions and lifestyles of today's seniors. Companies that hop on this will make a truckload of money. Here are some tips to help them get started.

The elderly are counseled to cut down on red meat and eat more fruits and vegetables. The first part of that prescription isn't too difficult to follow. Older teeth have a harder time chewing the sinews of red meat anyway. Our challenge is eating more vegetables, especially the frequently touted nightshades.

Imagine if cauliflower and Brussels sprouts, broccoli and even mushrooms had their DNA reconfigured to reduce the gas buildup in our GI tracts! As long as they're in the lab anyway, could scientists maybe give us some lettuce we can chew without having to cut it with a knife?

Geriatrics have a laundry list of beloved foods that could have their salt reduced. Top of my list would be the wonderful hard cheeses I crave every afternoon. And most evenings. And occasionally late mornings. It would be a plus if chemists could also reduce their fat level without diminishing the flavor.

Here's one that could present a challenge even to Nobel-prize-winning biologists. Get rid of the acid in tomatoes. I'm half Italian, so I love my sauce. Or as my aunts called it: gravy. (My mother married a non-Italian, so in our home, gravy was brown. If it was red, it was sauce.) I'll steam cauliflower and drown in it sauce-gravy as a healthy pasta substitute if I'm guaranteed a gas and reflux-free evening. Especially if I can top it with low-salt grated Parmesan.

Those of us with what I'll lump into the category of "architectural enhancements" to our teeth have other issues. My personal bugaboo is caps, but I'm sure that bridges and dentures behave the same, if not worse. All types of food get stuck in the crevices and under the edges. Sesame seeds aren't the only culprits that lurk there.

Take nuts, for instance. I love nuts and they're relatively healthy. But I'm picking and flossing the pieces for days after I eat them. Ditto for broiled chicken. Genetically modify to address this, and I will be putty in your non-latex gloved hands, Mr. Biochemist.

Every week I hear about some new health problem that's linked to inflammation and foods that cause it. It's not just the joint pain that comes with arthritis, an almost-inevitable consequence of aging. Heart disease is now reputed to be aggravated by foods that cause inflammation. These are frequently the same ones that contribute to high blood pressure and high cholesterol. By GMOing the inflammation inducers, we can knock off multiple geriatric ailments.

Since we can't fix all of those at once, let researchers focus on this manageable list: sugar and refined carbs, egg yolks, bacon, shrimp, butter, and the most popular cheeses. For the record, I've never liked bacon and I rarely eat mac and cheese. But I know these are comfort foods for the rest of the world, and I'm nothing if not considerate of my fellow retirees.

Finally, no post that touches on things that pass my lips would be complete without addressing wine. From my vantage point, there are two ways that GMOs could improve my *vino* experience. The first would be to alter the DNA of the sulfites that are used as preservatives in less expensive wines. It's not that I'm such a wine snob that I appreciate only the pricier vintages. OK. Maybe it is a little bit that. But it's more that sulfites make me sneeze and give me headaches.

While scientists are massaging the grapes, I'd appreciate whatever they can do to address one other senior pitfall of imbibing. That is, the alcohol-induced snooze. I'm not asking for much—just two glasses without having my eyelids start to droop.

Those who are adamantly opposed to having Genetically Modified Organisms in our food supply are probably cringing right now. But we of a certain age believe that Geriatrically Modified Organisms should earn their developers a "Noble" Prize. I'll drink to that.

Thresholds, Stairs and Memory Loss

Original Post Date Feb. 22, 2014

Retirement finds most of us spending more time in our homes, making us aware of how frequently we forget where we're headed when we go from one room to another. You might think this is magnified in our minds because we're home more often. Turns out, there's a scientific reason for this memory gap.

The University of Notre Dame published a study some years ago that has only now come to my attention. The author is Professor Gabriel Radvansky, and his ND webpage tells us his research *"is aimed at understanding... how younger and older adults differ on their use of mental models."* I'm sure this is a fascinating field, but I'm mostly interested in his paper: *"Walking through doorways causes forgetting."*

In that study, subjects either walked through a doorway to another room to get something, or they walked the same distance within a room. Those who crossed a threshold (what Radvansky calls an "event boundary") showed more memory loss than those who walked within a room. He concluded that these event boundaries compartmentalize activities in the mind, filing them in separate mental spaces. This impedes the ability to retrieve thoughts or decisions made in a different room.

His conclusion comes as no surprise to me. In fact, I can add to his findings. The more doorways you walk through, the harder it is to remember what you started out planning to do. We have a big house (please, Lord, not for much longer). I have things going on from the basement to the third floor and the two floors in between. I rarely get through a day without forgetting which floor I'm headed to, never mind for what reason. The further I have to go, the more likely I am to forget why before I get there.

Speaking of floors, stairs are another major "event boundary." If something requires me to hit the stairs, chances are I'm going to forget what it was that put me there. If I'm lucky enough to remember why I've arrived on an upper floor, I'll likely realize I left an important paper in the basement from whence I set out. Or I need a tool that's in a closet or drawer on a lower floor.

My cat Luke's nail clippers, for instance. He's usually on one of the second floor beds, but his clippers are in a cabinet off the kitchen. I'm not likely to forget why I'm carrying a bowl of his food upstairs. But it can take weeks before I put the notion of carrying the clippers with me into the equation. Note to self: why not store an extra pair of clippers in the linen closet between the bedrooms? Second note to self: remember where you just put that first note.

I think I know why stairs are such a major contributor to forgetfulness, other than Radvansky's research or Murphy's Law. It has to do with this charming A. A. Milne poem:

Half way down the stairs is a stair where I sit.
There isn't any other stair quite like it.
I'm not at the bottom; I'm not at the top.
So this is the stair where I always stop.
Halfway up the stairs isn't up and it isn't down.
It isn't in the nursery; it isn't in the town.
And all sorts of funny thoughts run round my head.
It isn't really anywhere! It's someplace else instead!

There you have it. We lose our minds on stairs because when we get halfway from here to there we're nowhere. And our minds are happy to join us there.

This leads to the conclusion that the best way to deal with these event boundaries is to eliminate them from our homes. In other words, when we retire, we should adopt an open floor plan: one enormous room with no doorways and no stairs. My husband loves that loft-style architecture. Me, not so much.

If you're giving this careful thought, you've probably realized that there needs to be at least one door: to the bathroom. Chances are, we won't forget why we were headed there, no matter how many trips we make in a day. For most of us, that's one thing to be thankful for. Of course, when we come out of the bathroom, figuring out where to go back to is something else entirely. That's what sticky notes are for. Note to self: Add post-it notes to shopping list.

Improving Mental Health

Original Post Date Apr. 5, 2014

Two posts that appeared on Facebook dealt with improving one's mental health. Since I love cashews and I used to knit, I'd consider using both of these to improve my mental well-being. But first I'd need to research the reports touting them, to evaluate the science.

The first article, from *www.naturalcuresnotmedicine.com*, claims that cashews are a natural antidepressant. This is good news for proponents of the holistic approach (and my life is full of them). Dave Sommers is cited for this quote: *"Two handfuls of cashews is [sic] the therapeutic equivalent of a prescription dose of Prozac."* He maintains that the L-tryptophan in cashews is converted to niacin and serotonin to reduce anxiety.

Best I can tell, this is true, so Eli Lilly must have staff looking to discredit it. I can picture some of the headlines: *"Cashews breed rare worm that burrows into your intestines."* Or: *"Fatty oils in cashews cause blockage of arteries; lead to increased risk of stroke."* Maybe Lilly doesn't care, since generic Prozac (fluoxetine) has now been approved by the FDA. Let those suppliers panic over cashew encroachment.

In any case, we now have this terrific alternative to prescription drugs to provide positive mind-altering benefits. And we don't have to smoke it to get them. Not only do I plan to eat more cashews (I had cut down on them because of my diet), I also plan to market my own brand. I'll call it *Mellow Yellow.*

The second article puts forth the notion that *"knitting is healthy for your brain."* The site *Jezebel.com* tells us several studies support this assertion, and that not just knitting, but any crafting provides these benefits. The specifics are so, well... specific, that I'm compelled to quote the full claim. Knitting *"serves as a natural anti-depressant, helps ease anxiety and stress, can protect your brain from aging and has the [same] effects as meditation."*

This news was so energizing that it sent me straight to my basement storage room looking for my knitting needles that were packed away when we staged the house for sale. No luck with that, but they'll show up eventually.

Jezebel.com cites a CNN series "Inside Your Brain" that credits knitting with treating PTSD, saying it "dampens internal chaos." I can't tell you how many times I've lamented: "I sure wish I had a way to dampen this internal chaos today." Claremont University Professor of Psychology Mihaly Csikszentmihalyi attributes this to something he refers to as "flow," which he calls *"the secret to happiness."* CNN says he has decades of research to support this.

The Claremont website describes the avuncular MC (as I prefer to call him) as *"the founder and co-director of the*

Quality of Life Research Center. The QLRC is a non-profit research institute that studies 'positive psychology'; that is, human strengths such as optimism, creativity, intrinsic motivation..." Plus he's a member of the National Academy of Leisure Studies. Who knew there even was such an academy? I'm now sufficiently impressed.

In a 2004 TED talk, MC said your existence outside a creative activity, such as knitting, becomes *"temporarily suspended"* and your sense of your body disappears. I don't know about you, but there are plenty of days when I wish my sense of my body would disappear. I'll knit one of those Snuggler body blankets if that will make it happen. Note to self: buy knitting needles if they don't show up soon.

Jezebel.com also cites a study published in the *British Journal of Occupational Therapy* that bolsters the CNN story and MC's findings. The study sounds credible, especially since the survey had over 3,500 respondents. Except that it was conducted online through an Internet knitting site. For all we know, 3,000 of those "knitters" were using their prison library to participate. Or 100 bored widows took the survey 35 times each.

Respondents said they knit for relaxation and stress relief; they also praised knitting in a group. (The prison library doesn't sound that far fetched now, does it?) The study thus concluded that: *"Knitting has significant psychological and social benefits, which can contribute to wellbeing and quality of life."* It seems to me that if you're in for life, it doesn't take much to improve its quality. Ditto for bored widows.

So the Brits leave me skeptical, but Professor MC seems credible. They don't let just anybody give a TED talk, you know. I have a vision of myself, nestled in the corner of our sunroom, humming Donovan tunes and knitting argyle socks by the basketful. I'm shoving fistfuls of cashews into my pie hole and I'm as happy as that proverbial clam. I'll call you when your socks are ready. In the meantime, be on the lookout for my Mellow Yellow. No prescription needed.

In Search of the
Perfect Lawn Chair

Original Post Date Jun. 7, 2014

Summer's almost here. It's time to drag the patio furniture from the basement storage and tune up the barbecue grill. Or maybe your furniture is kept overhead in the garage and you're a fan of cold salads. Either way, you're probably thinking about replacing some of your seasonal seating.

Whether it's in the front yard, on the back deck or in a sunny spot at the local shore, there's a place in everyone's summer life where they like to stretch out on a comfortable lawn chair. Notice that we call it a "lawn" chair even if it sits on a slate patio, a wooden pallet or a sandy beach. The more time you spend on it, the more you appreciate the importance of finding the perfect lawn chair.

When I was working full time, this wasn't a major concern. I sat down so infrequently on weekends that an aluminum folding chair with missing webbing was just fine. Or one of those stackable plastic ones you find in the promotional aisle at the supermarket every Spring. Now that I'm retired and we're ready to downsize, I expect to spend a lot of time relaxing outdoors. This realization sent me in search of the perfect lawn chair.

My first stop was one of those pseudo-hardware stores that load up on seasonal supplies, changing much of their stock four times a year. I tried out updated versions of my webbed aluminum beach chair. One model had straps so narrow that they cut into my ample fanny, leaving parts of me drooping through the gaps. Another one, with wider straps, had no give at all, which meant no air circulation. Not a good design for the hot sun.

I found one with webbing that seemed just right, so I sat down. Because I'm short (one half inch shorter than last year, according to my GP), my feet didn't touch the ground unless I pointed my toes, giving me a cramp. A similarly-webbed option looked closer to the ground. When I tried it out, I discovered it was too close to Mother Earth. My knees accordioned under my chin and I had to tip the chair on its side to get out of it.

I headed to a larger home goods store that had an entire section devoted to patio and garden needs. Not a single chair there had webbing or an aluminum frame. This boded well. Instead we had "genuine California redwood" and "environmentally-sensitive repurposed plastic." Be still my heart.

I jumped right into phase two of my assessment process: adjusting the tilt. I picked a friendly looking chair and set it at a promising angle before I sat down. I was pleased that my feet reached the ground yet my knees didn't hit my chin (or boobs). The angle I'd chosen was fine if I planned to read, but I needed to lean back more if I wanted to take a nap.

I moved the tilt lever (carefully, I thought) and instantly I was flat on my back with my shirtsleeve caught in the lever. I was virtually immobile. After about ten minutes, another shopper wandered by and rescued me. Being the adventurous type, I tried out several more loungers, with similar results. About an hour later (and after my fourth rescue), I decided to go back to the drawing board.

By drawing board, I mean my car, in which I drove to a specialty retailer that carries nothing but summer furniture. Here I discovered another criterion to narrow the choices in my search for the perfect lawn chair: price. My budget eliminated three-quarters of the stock displayed so invitingly throughout the store. At least I had an attentive employee to help untangle me if necessary.

Speaking of help, my salesperson asked an unexpected question: *"Have you ever considered a hammock?"* I resisted the urge to ask: *"Have you considered having your head examined?"* Instead I answered meekly: *"My joints are creaky. I have zero core strength and even less balance. Do you have a hammock that addresses those issues?"* It turns out he did not. But what he did have was the perfect lawn chair for me.

When I first sat down, I was practically standing up. I pushed a button and it gently set me at just the right level for my height. I pushed another button, and it tilted me back for a snooze. It came with a waterproof cover and a spare power pack. It even had (wait for it…) a special cup holder for my wine cooler!

It also came with a price tag that placed it well into that three-quarters of their stock above my budget. I bought it anyway. Let's face it. The perfect lawn chair is priceless.

In Search of the
Perfect Sunglasses

Original Post Date Sep. 6, 2014

September may seem an odd time to write about sunglasses, but my friend, Sid, has pointed out that seniors should protect their eyes with sunglasses all year long. Also, I was on posting hiatus all summer while I was in housing (and Internet) limbo. That's when one of the morning TV shows ran a feature on sunglasses, so I had to hold the topic 'til now.

The hosts modeled a variety of designs, from aviators to oversized "glamour" styles. I recognized many of them as looks I've worn over the years. Some dated back to the sixties and early seventies and could best be described as retro-hippie. Others were inspired by celebrities who popularized them via publicity shots for a hit movie or in a "selfie" posted on Instagram.

The TV segment made me realize that the needs I have now in sunglasses are vastly different from what I looked for in my earlier years. While I'm attracted to ones that are stylish, I've reached the "function vs. form" stage of my life. It's not important for me to look trendy. What's essential is that I don't trip or bump into things when I'm wearing them and that I'm not blinded by the midday sun. There are a few additional requirements that I look for in the perfect sunglasses.

One thing I can't stand in any type of glasses is rims that block vision clarity. I don't want to keep looking to the side to see what's there when it's actually the frames that are distracting me. Likewise, I don't want to have to keep tipping my head up or down so the upper edge isn't smack in the middle of the wine label I'm trying to read. I'm not a bobble-head doll.

A related pet peeve is openings on the sides of sunglasses that let glare in. This means that some amount of wrap-around is in order. But at our age, we're no Bono. We're not even Bono-wannabes. Our mantra is "everything in moderation." Well, everything except wine, that is.

Speaking of age, bifocals are important, even in sunglasses, but they shouldn't be visibly bi. I want to wear the same pair when I'm reading a book by the pool as I do when I'm driving. If I need two separate pairs, I'm bound to get them mixed up. I'll be wondering why I have to hold the book so far away to read the print and why I have to lean over the steering wheel to see what's in front of my car. I've done dual-pairs-on-dueling-leashes before and I almost strangled myself more than once. It wasn't pretty.

Also along the lines of dual functions, the automatic transition from outdoors to indoors would be helpful. We make plenty of trips to the bathroom at our age. A quick changeover from sunlight to a darker room would be a plus, since we won't always have time to take off our sunglasses before we head to the loo. If you've ever sneezed when looking into the sun, you know what I'm talking about.

Moving on to cosmetic issues, the sunglasses must be light enough so they don't leave a ridge on the bridge of my nose, or skin flaps on its sides. My mother had those marks from wearing her regular glasses all the time. When working indoors, I check my nose in the mirror several times a day. If I see even a hint of a ridge or a flap, I massage in some Nivea and take the glasses off for a spell. I'm not vain enough to carry a mirror around outside, so my sunglasses will have to prevent this problem on their own merit.

Those of us of a certain age need sunglasses of moderate size, regardless of whatever is the current trend. They can't be too big. We're not Sophia Loren or Elton John, after all. And they can't be too small. We're also not Yoko Ono or Benjamin Franklin. The best way to be sure you're picking a "moderate" size is to lay out a group of glasses that meet all the other above requirements. Then throw out the largest and the smallest ones. What's left should be acceptable.

Finally, the perfect sunglasses must be affordably priced without doing one of those "buy-one-get-second-pair-at half-off" deals that usually wind up costing more than twice what buying just one should cost. I'm not looking for something from the dollar store. I just don't want the cost eating into my wine budget. After all, not even a perfect pair of sunglasses is worth giving up a nice bottle of *Chianti Classico*.

Section VII

Wistful Reflections

Go Ahead... Make His Day

Original Post Date Jun. 8, 2013

When I was young, let's say in my twenties and early thirties, I was fly. And, truth be told, pretty hot. Lunchtime often saw me out and about in midtown Manhattan in miniskirts and high heels. It was not unusual for construction workers to make admiring comments, catcalls and an occasional suggestion that cannot be repeated here. Actually, most of the comments can't be repeated here, either. Looking back, I realize that it felt good to be appreciated, regardless of the source.

Unless my memory has huge gaps, decades went by without any catcalls. The only appreciative comments I remember from my forties and fifties were compliments on my perfume. I got those quite regularly, from both men and women. The men often asked the name of it, so they could buy it for their wives or girlfriends. It was Issey, by Issey Miyake, by the way, and my niece, Pam, is the one who hooked me on it.

Then there was one memorable encounter about six years ago, while I was still working. Once a year, I spent a few days at a local senior center that had what was called an RSVP operation. The center received a government grant in exchange for providing free help with bulk mailings for non-profit groups. The women who frequented the center did the folding, assembling and stuffing.

I checked in periodically to replenish materials and to make sure things were being done according to spec. I was usually dressed in what would best be described as casual business wear—a soft skirt and blouse or sweater. One day as I was leaving, I crossed paths with an elderly gentleman; he was probably in his eighties. He said something complimentary— I can't recall exactly what—and I smiled and thanked him. I would have hugged him, but one has to worry about the tickers in older gents.

I was reminded of this encounter recently as I was about to pull out of a Home Depot parking lot. A man in his late fifties, or perhaps his sixties—I can't tell ages anymore—was walking from his car to the store. He was balding. Actually, he was almost completely bald. He had a paunch, but not a sloppy one; his golf-type shirt was tucked neatly into his belted sports slacks. With spine erect, he walked purposefully through the lot. He looked confident, but not arrogant.

I was so impressed to see someone of this vintage with good posture and energy that I almost rolled down my car window to say something to him. "Looking good!" Or perhaps "I admire your posture and the way you walk so briskly." I wasn't sure what I should say, so instead, I just drove away. Besides, I was afraid he'd think I was hitting on him. (I'm not fly anymore, so he certainly wouldn't have considered my attentions flattering.)

Before I even reached the street, I regretted that I didn't pay him a compliment. He deserved it. He had earned one. I knew that fly or not, anything I would have said would have lifted the spirits of this seemingly ordinary man. I could have made his day, but instead I chickened out. That's when I remembered the senior gent who had perked me up a few years back.

So, here's my advice to everyone reading this. If you see someone who looks good or is doing something nice, go ahead... make his day! Let him (or her) know that you've noticed. "Way to rock it!" "You look mah-velous!" (*a la* Billy Crystal). "You smell awesome!" "Love your shoes!" "Somebody's been working out!" I could go on, but you get the idea.

Are you too shy to speak up to a stranger? Then give them a big smile, or just a head nod. You'd be surprised how easy it can be to lift someone's spirits for a few hours, or even for the entire day. Try it. I promise it will make you feel good, too.

By the way, you look great today!

Forever Homes Together
Original Post Date Oct. 26, 2013

Most of us who have adopted a pet from a shelter are familiar with the expression "forever home." It's the ultimate goal for every rescued animal—to become part of a family where they will be loved and cared for forever.

When the time comes for them to leave us, we may have our four-legged children buried in a pet cemetery. It's also not unusual to have them cremated and the ashes returned to us to be kept in special commemorative urns and boxes.

Less often, we make plans to keep them with us after we've likewise headed into the sunset. I read about a woman who wanted her pet buried with her despite a local ordinance that prohibited it. She had the cat cremated and she sewed the ashes into the hem of her wedding gown. She left instructions to bury her in that gown, thus ensuring that she and Fluffy would be together forever.

One of my friends had several months to prepare for her departure from us. She was buried in the Jewish tradition, wrapped in cotton in a plain wooden box. Before she died, she found a sympathetic rabbi who allowed the ashes of her dog, who predeceased her, to be slipped into the coffin next to her. They're now in their forever home together. Knowing this was pre-arranged gave my friend comfort in her last weeks.

The *New York Daily News* ran an article about a successful court challenge to a related regulation. Pet owners in New York State were prevented from having their ashes interred in pet cemeteries next to their family companions. The niece of a NYPD officer brought the suit on behalf of her deceased uncle. The man's wife had already been buried next to their dogs in a Hartsdale pet cemetery.

It's not clear whether the cemetery had been ignoring an existing statute, or whether the prohibition was newly enacted into law. Either way, hundreds of deceased pet owners were already resting there with their Mittens and their Scouts. The niece won the suit and her uncle's ashes are now interred next to his wife's and those of their three pooches.

This has me wondering about my own future disposition. I plan to be cremated, as does my husband (after the medical school at Brown University has finished studying him). Neither of us has decided what should happen to our ashes, except to be scattered somewhere. I suppose we should be blown away as a family, even though that would involve storing the cremains of one of us until the other catches up. Now I'm thinking that our girls and Luke (still purring) should be tossed out with us.

I commissioned custom pottery jars to hold the urns with the ashes of my first "girls," Daisy Hyacinth and Tulip Wisteria. The front of one jar has a molded daisy, the other a molded tulip. The lids have those flowers etched into the undersides. (If they're looking up, they'll know they're in the correct jar.) I have these on a shelf in the sunroom. Most visitors have no idea what's in them.

The ashes of my second two, Pansy Gardenia and Lily Magnolia, are in cedar boxes. (The vet used a different  cremation service and my potter was no longer potting.) The boxes are tied with ribbons that have antique floral pins— a pansy and a calla lily— attached. I keep them on the dresser in our bedroom.

So, what to do with all these cremains (ours included) when the time comes? Sprinkling them into the ocean or a lake isn't a good idea. Cats don't like water. We could run an ad on Craig's List. "Wanted. Service to scatter ashes of family of 7 from top of mountain somewhere in Northeast." Or maybe book a hot air balloon ride for a friend who loves pets and could sneak a large satchel of dust into the passenger basket.

One of my more extreme ideas is to mix us with Elmer's glue to make trinkets that would get stuffed inside a large piñata. There must be some fresh air camp with kids who'd benefit from releasing their pent up aggression. Or we could pre-arrange a picnic in a park and sell tickets to take a swing at us. Lots of folks would pay good money to whack me with a stick. (Proceeds to a local shelter, of course.)

Somewhere in here is an idea with legs. And even if not, we should have quite a few years before we need to figure this out. It won't matter where our forever home is as long as we're together (sing along now) *side by side.*

I'm Six Again At Christmastime

Original Post Date Dec. 27, 2013

With the Christmas season upon us I'm in high gear. It's one of my favorite times of the year. Our family has cut down on gift giving, which enables us to focus on the warm and fuzzy stuff. Since Jagdish and I will be downsizing to a condo next year, I'm taking advantage of the ample space that our house offers to put out more holiday décor than usual.

I have an entire closet filled with almost nothing but house and tree decorations. The first things out are the snowmen and Santa-like items. This year, I found myself talking to them as I placed them throughout the rooms. It dawned on me that it's like I become six again at Christmastime.

Hello, Italian snowman (round belly, red and green hat) with your Chanukah snowman friend (blue clothes). Hey, Humpty Dumpty Santa and Mrs. Humpty Claus. How was your summer? Snowman family on the piano, are the kids going to college soon? I don't care that they never answer me. I move on to the next grouping. There's the Laurel and Hardy snowmen—one super thin, the other round as a pumpkin. Or maybe they're Jagdish and Elaine.

It's Christmastime and I'm 26 again. I'm unwrapping an ornament my father gave me for one of my first trees living on my own. It's a brass mask from Venezuela, still in the  tissue and plastic bag it came in. My father asked a co-worker going there on a business trip to bring back something appropriate for a tree ornament for him to give me. He was hugely disappointed in the mask. I think he was expecting a star. I always loved it, especially because of the story behind it. His name, spelled wrong by his co-worker, is still penciled onto the tissue.

It's Christmastime and in my mind I'm 39. I'm unpacking the silver snowflakes and brass stars from the Metropolitan Museum gift shop. My parents gave me one each year, but my father picked them out. I'm missing the one for 1984. He died that year. My mother wanted to get the ornament for me, but it was just too painful for her to deal with. It was painful for me, too. I started buying them on my own the next year. In my collection over a 31-year period, the only year missing is the one my father died.

I'm baking Sunset Cookies from my mother's recipe. I'm 50 and it's my first Christmas without her. These cookies remind me of her. If I made struffoli, I'd feel even closer. She made the dough and rolled it into finger-width strands. I cut them into dice-sized pieces. After they were fried, she drizzled them with honey and I formed the ring around an upside down glass. When we removed the glass, we decorated with colored sprinkles and her "Italian" plastic holly. I don't have a deep fryer, so I make her cookies.

I've reached my 68th Christmas. I'm cranky. I have very little patience. I say things that aren't appropriate to repeat here to people who don't put on their left turn signal and just stop dead in the fast lane, waiting to make the turn. Also to those who drive behind me as I'm backing out of a parking spot in the supermarket lot, even though I'm already more than half way out. I back up ever so slowly, because I know some idiot is going to be in a hurry to get the cantaloupe that's on sale yet again this week.

I silently give thanks that our family has cut way back on the exchange of presents and that almost everyone is on a diet. But it's still Christmas, so I put up three trees. That includes the little artificial one that is now Luke's, but is full of ornaments bought for Tulip and Daisy and Lily and Pansy. Bittersweet memories.

We've been in our house on Oriole Avenue for 22 Christmases. Each of the last three years, I've considered the possibility that it could be our final Christmas here. It makes me sad, but I remind myself that Christmas is not a physical place. It's a place in one's mind and in one's heart. No matter where we relocate, I'll be able to unpack Christmas from my ornament boxes and bake it from my recipe file. If I can just remember where I put the patience I had when I was younger, it will be as perfect as when I was six.

Memories of Marijuana—
Or Dreams?

Original Post Date Jan. 11, 2014

Some of the early headlines of 2014 feature the legalization of marijuana. Colorado now allows the statewide retail sale of small amounts for "recreational use" and Washington State is ready to join them. New York's governor is considering easing that state's restrictions on the medical use of cannabis. *Time* magazine predicts more states will follow these leads. *(Midterm elections in November 2014 saw Alaska, Oregon and Washington D. C. also legalizing personal use of weed.)*

Hard as it may be to believe, I've never smoked marijuana. Not one puff. I therefore have difficulty visualizing the amount of Mary Jane that would qualify as recreational. Oh sure, I attended parties in Greenwich Village in the late sixties where joints were being passed around. But there were always enough strangers toking to prevent me from trying it. I've always been a control freak and I wasn't about to loosen up unless I was surrounded by people I knew I could trust.

My brother, Rick, was stationed in Germany around that time as part of his ROTC commitment. After he was discharged, he and some friends crossed Northern Africa in a Volkswagon bus/camper. His travels included Morocco and the Canary Islands. You can probably see where this is headed.

When he returned to the States he lived with me briefly in Manhattan. I learned to burn incense to cover the smell of his ganja. I worried that my upscale neighbors would send New York's finest to the door of my brownstone studio. That's about as close as I got to actually smoking weed.

My brother, though a year older than I, followed my early career path into computer programming. He worked for a time at Sears & Roebuck, where he bought a water pipe with his employee discount. That seemed as bizarre to me as if someone were to get mail-order contraceptives thru Reader's Digest. (Remember, this was the sixties.) I began buying incense by the bundle.

After several months, Rick got his own apartment in the East Village. I still saw him regularly at the Spanish lessons we took together. These began in Midtown, at the Latin American Institute, and eventually migrated to Flushing, Queens, where our instructor lived. By coincidence, I also lived in Flushing at that point, with my first husband. When the formal lessons ended, my brother and I engaged Sr. Alfaro for private ones once a week. Rick drove us there after work.

I remember one night, going across the 59th Street bridge. We heard a siren behind us. "I hope we don't get pulled over," my brother said, off-handedly. "What makes you say that?" I asked. "You're sitting on half a key," he explained. My first thought was: "Why would the cops care if I had a key under my fanny?" And then: "What the hell does *half* a key open?"

When Rick explained that was short for "kilo," as in kilogram (of MJ), I broke out into a cold sweat. "Honest, officer," I imagined myself saying. "I didn't even know it was there, plus I've never smoked it in my life." Yeah, right. Hair to my waist, skirt up to my gotcha, next to my "brother" who looked nothing like me. So that was it. I'd go to the big house for something I didn't do, without even having had the benefit of ever getting high.

As the years wore on, I would occasionally catch a whiff of marijuana smoke as I walked through midtown Manhattan. And later on sidewalks on Providence's East Side. One evening last summer, I got light-headed sitting in our sunroom, with the windows cranked wide open. I discovered that my neighbor's college-age son and his friends were sitting on their back deck, smoking. I suppressed the urge to call over, "I know what you're doing."

After awhile, I closed the windows. It was too ironic to imagine myself getting high alone, in my late sixties, after having avoided doing it with strangers in *the* late sixties. Which brings me back to recent headlines.

My mother suffered from glaucoma and my eyes are checked for it regularly. A friend pointed out the upside if I ever get that diagnosis. I could smoke pot legally now that medical marijuana dispensaries are open in Rhode Island. I prefer to consider options with my eyes healthy. I can visit friends in Colorado, and maybe eventually in New York. Hell, one of my classmates has a home in both states. (What did she know that the rest of us didn't?)

Maybe when my friends and I turn 70 we'll have a big girls' slumber party. We'll call it "MJ In Your PJs." Kind of gives new meaning to "Sweet Dreams," doesn't it? I'll bring the brownie mix. And lots of incense.

Weight Loss Wardrobes

Original Post Date Feb. 15, 2014

The number that the scale recorded at last year's annual physical shocked me into the realization that I needed to lose weight. A lot of weight. Knowing that it gets harder and harder to accomplish this the older we get, I decided it was time to develop a plan. My goal was to lose 30 pounds before my mid-year checkup and another 10 to 15 by the next annual physical. I came close, losing 28 by mid-year; there's still three months 'til my annual. Along the way, I learned some things about weight loss and wardrobes.

Some of the discoveries were good news; some not so great. On the plus side (or not so plus anymore), my calves are finally sized for regular width boots. Before the diet, I could fit into only the wide width styles, but those were so wide, it looked like I was wearing funnels on my legs. So, I stopped wearing high boots, traded them for mukluks and muttered to myself "function over form." On the minus side, I tossed my regular width boots when I de-cluttered the house to list it, so I'm still wearing mukluks.

Staying with footwear, I also learned that being thinner means my taller socks last longer. Before the diet, my calves stretched out the elastic at the top of my socks within a season. The socks then slipped down into puddles at my ankles. The good news is that with my newly slimmed legs, the elastic in my high socks will last for years. The bad news is that if I diet until I reach my goal, my calves may get so slim the socks will fall down anyway. Garters, anyone?

Moving up my body to slacks, I'm down about two sizes over all, though my waist is apparently on a different schedule from the rest of me. As with the boots, I got rid of much of my too-small wardrobe in preparation for our downsizing. I did save a few pairs of favorite slacks in hopes I could squeeze into them again someday. As it happens, most of those are summer weight.

I need to paint a picture here of how my pants fit as my weight goes up and down. The ideal look is to have them drape in a way that tastefully sculpts my behind. When I put on a few pounds, we get more of a clutching than sculpting. At my extreme weight, the pants were clinging for dear life. Needless to say, I was looking forward to having things fit more tastefully again.

This week I decided to visit the cedar closet on our third floor; that's where I store my off-season wardrobe. Spring will be here in two or three months and I wanted to see what might fit me this year. I found two pairs of pants that I had kept in the "hope springs eternal" section of the closet. With great anticipation, I tried them on. Keep in mind that there is snow on the ground, and more coming. So there's no chance of wearing these yet.

Imagine my dismay when I discovered that my lower torso had passed right through "drape" to "droop" where these beloved pants were concerned. They're passable enough for me to wear them now (barely), but now is not when I need summer weight clothes. Who knows how bad the droop will be after two or three more months of dieting? I refuse to give up on them, however, and I'm considering investing in one of those "Kim Kardashian" butt enhancers that you see on late-night TV.

I'm faring better with some of my favorite jackets. In addition to dieting, I've been using hand weights most mornings. My hope is to get some definition to my upper arms and avoid that bat-wing look that we older women get. Extreme weight loss can lead to excess flesh, so if you've got it, *don't* flaunt it. I doubt I'll be running around sleeveless anytime soon, although you never know. Read on.

One of the other articles of clothing nostalgia in that "hope springs eternal" section was a tank top from Club Med. It has a visual pun on the front, and the explanation (in French) on the back. I couldn't bear to part with it. There's a certain allure to French women, after all, even when they're Italian. The tank doesn't go with those pants that droop, but maybe I'll wear it with them anyway. Perhaps it will direct peoples' eyes upwards. But if that Kardashian butt enhancer does its job, I'll probably keep my jacket on.

Hope does indeed spring eternal.

Write What You Know.
Or Not.

Original Post Date Apr. 26, 2014

A lecture on memoirs that I attended with some friends was cancelled about half way through because of a health emergency in the audience. While we were waiting for a decision on whether the event would continue, we chatted about what we're writing. One friend is penning memoirs about his family members. The other is working on fiction based on her recently deceased dog. I continue to write essays in my signature style: self-deprecating social satire.

I said I didn't think I could do fiction, that I wouldn't be good at it. The memoir friend said he thought I should give it a try. At about that point, the organizers postponed the lecture, to be rescheduled at some date to be determined, and our little group disbanded.

Since then, I've given some thought to writing fiction. We've all heard the advice: "Write what you know." As a marketer, I would add to that: "Write what people want to read." Note that I did not say: "Write what people will buy." I'm in the camp that believes that if you're writing to sell your work or to get on the morning talk shows, you're writing for the wrong reasons.

With that in mind, I wondered what readers are interested in this year. To that end, I looked at the latest issue of *Publishers*

Weekly. Because my husband carries some books in his store, he receives *PW*, and he brings it home for me to read. The April 21 issue has a section on self-publishing (my method of getting into print), and "the thriving romance and erotica categories" in particular. Oh, my.

If writing what I know that is now a hot button (pardon the pun) means romance and erotica, I'm in big trouble. To be sure, I have plenty to draw upon in that genre from my (misspent) youth. But I wouldn't want anyone who came into my life from my mid-thirties onward to read "fiction" based on my salad days.

To further that analogy, we're not talking iceberg lettuce and those uniform hothouse tomatoes that come end-to-end in a plastic tray. My bowl would have the most colorful and diverse maché imaginable. And a mixture of beefsteaks, Italian plums and those little grape tomatoes that scoot off the plate when you try to put your fork into them. Oh, and at least one Mr. Stripey.

It would also have English cucumbers (not your standard garden ones), several types and colors of radishes and a wide variety of olives. You'd probably find at least one carrot (peeled, with the ends trimmed, but not sliced...) Are you beginning to get the picture?

This puts me in mind of a long ago exchange with a close female friend back when I worked in Manhattan. We'd both (separately) seen the porn movie *The Devil in Miss Jones*. Excuse me. I meant art film. *"I bet you'll never eat a banana again,"* I joked. *"Bananas, yes,"* she replied. *"Grapes, no."*

Those of you hoping this post continues to go downhill will be disappointed. I'm not ready to share the salient details of those years. That will require a skilled therapist to draw out the deeply-suppressed memories from my subconscious. I'll also need to come up with an appropriate pseudonym under which to publish that genre of fiction.

I'll pass on the first names Johanna, Marilyn and Georgina. And I certainly won't take the last name Green or Grey. I suppose my pen name should be arcane or provocative. Maybe *Balsam Gardner*. That would be a head nod to my salad days and to the vinegar I prefer. Or perhaps *Saucy Salsa*. That provides some colorful *double entendres* to chew on.

If you find a novel in the erotica section by an author who sounds like she's been tossed around in a well-oiled wooden bowl, it might be my first attempt at undercover fiction (again, pardon the pun). Note the operative word "fiction." One thing's for certain. It won't be titled: *The Story of E*.

Retirement Sparks Redux

Acknowledgments

I could not get any *Retirement Sparks* book to print without the help of my proofreading stalwarts:

> Becky Eckstein, Joe Petteruti and my
> husband, Jagdish Sachdev.

By now, they've resigned themselves to being called upon every year or two to perform this service for me. Jagdish doesn't have much choice. But Becky and Joe... Well, as the song goes: *That's what friends are for!*

I just hope I don't wear out my welcome.

About the Author

Elaine M. Decker is a social satirist and a recovering Type-A personality. A New Jersey native (when Jersey wasn't cool), she relocated to Providence, RI in 1992 (when Providence wasn't cool, either). In 2014, she and her husband and remaining cat downsized to a condo in Cromwell, CT.

After graduating from Brown University, Ms. Decker lived and worked in the metro NY area for 25 years. Following an early career in computer programming and systems, she climbed a Fortune 500 ladder into consumer marketing. From there she dabbled in communications, producing videos and creating websites. Continuing on what was clearly a logically thought out career path, she migrated into development and nonprofit management. She recently retired to devote more time to her writing and to refining her napping techniques.

One of her essays is included in *70 Things To Do When You Turn 70*. Her work has appeared in *The New York Times*, *Marketing News* and *The Privacy Journal*. Her retirement column appears in the RI publication, *Prime Time*. You can read her weekly blog at *retirementsparks.blogspot.com*.